The Business & Politics
of Sports
A Selection of Columns

The Business & Politics of Sports
A Selection of Columns

by Evan Weiner

TBE Press
New Canaan, Connecticut
2005

The Business & Politics of Sports:
A Selection of Columns by Evan Weiner
Copyright © 2005 Evan Weiner

Published by TBE Press
An imprint of TBM Records
Post Office Box 1656
New Canaan, CT 06840
www.bickley.com

Author Photograph by Tom Hughey
Cover Design by Linda Clark
Book Design by Elizabeth A. Dean

ISBN: 1-883210-05-4
Library of Congress Control Number: 2005903429

Manufactured in the United States of America

For my wife Brenda who has put up with me for all these years and for my children Megan and Jarred who are the best two children that a father can ask for.

Contents

Endorsement/Sponsorship

Labor

Events

Politics

Media

Stadiums

Acknowledgments

Special thanks to the late Dr. James McCarthy my favorite college teacher for teaching me to speak and enunciate; to Peter Carey for teaching me that I may think that I'm smart but smartness doesn't count when you are a writer, it's hard work and research that counts; to Spencer Rumsey at *Newsday* for believing in what I do and giving me a chance; to Ted Fay at Cortland State University in New York who encouraged me to do this project; to Thomas P. Rosandich, Ph.D., President and CEO, United States Sports Academy, for his kindness and confidence in me; to Lou Hebert for giving me a soapbox for my commentaries in 1999; to Dewey Knutsen for his help in 1998 and 1999; to my childhood and lifelong friend, the late Roger Benima who watched everything unfold with a laugh and who left us far, far too early in life; to Tanya Bickley who put in a lot of effort and for seeing this project through; to Elizabeth Dean and Linda Clark for their efforts in this book; and to all the others along the way.

Preface

About two years ago I was talking to an Op-Ed page editor in Pittsburgh about the politics of sports business and the Atlantic Coast Conference's bold move of offering ACC membership to three Big East schools. The editor thought there might be a day in which sports issues would be on his Op-Ed pages. But today wasn't that day, although he could see the merit of opinion pieces on how sports really operate.

That is the mindset of newspaper and magazine editors, along with radio and TV programmers. Sports are merely games; the toy store of life. Nothing to be taking seriously. After all, seven-year-olds play sports.

The mindset is wrong. More than ever, sports is a business. A multi-billion dollar business with global implications. General Electric is spending billions of dollars so that its NBC-TV network can broadcast the 2010 and 2012 Olympics. Communities all over America have created special tax districts, raised hotel, motel, rent-a-car, restaurant, cigarette, and beer taxes to fund stadiums and arenas. Congress may take up discrimination legislation against men-only member golf courses, change tax exemption laws as they apply to companies that are Olympic sponsors, and legislate the boxing industry. The House Committee on Government Reform has held hearings on sports leagues drug testing, specifically testing for anabolic steroids.

Those issues aren't found in the sandbox or the playground. That's why the mindset has to be changed. Sure, sports journalism tackles some issues; frivolous ones like, "Is Bud Selig a Good Baseball Commissioner or is He-Bud-Lite?" And, sure, a talking head like Bob Costas will try to intellectualize the "Is He Good or Bud Lite?" debate. But people need to be aware of just how government influences the sporting industry and its cause and effect.

Without the change in the 1986 Tax Code, new stadiums and arenas would never have been built. The mass expansion of the 1980s and 1990s would never have had happened. The tax code change allowed municipalities to become very involved in public-private sponsorships of sports. Sports is a business with labor actions that sometimes are settled amicably and other times not. It depends on government funding for facilities, for cable TV regulation or deregulation, and tax breaks for corporations who buy tickets as a business expense and write-off. Sports also needs watchdogs. The industry has very few of them looking into the actual day-to-day operations of the business.

Colleges are offering sports business management courses because it's a growing field. Editors and programmers need to look at sports as more than an entertainment forum. Journalists also need to examine the sports industry because, in the end, just about every American citizen has some money directly or indirectly invested in the sports industry.

That's why we need more competent journalists taking a closer look. It's great to watch a game and report on it, but democracy deserves more than a box score when it comes to scrutinizing the business of sports.

— Evan Weiner
August 2005

Business

Is the NHL Healthy or Skating on Thin Ice?

The National Sports Weekly, January 1998

Boston Bruins president Harry Sinden complained about the skyrocketing costs of operating a National Hockey League franchise after he took part in the league's annual winter meetings in Arizona.

Sinden noted that NHL teams are spending 72 percent of their revenues to pay players. The game is in bad shape because of that, according to Sinden, who was a "Hawk" during the NHL lockout at the start of the 1994–95 season. He also indicated that ticket sales alone can no longer support operating costs of teams.

Sinden's comments may have caught NHL Commissioner Gary Bettman off guard. Bettman has a number of other front burner problems, namely the Pittsburgh Penguins' bankruptcy and the NHL Players' Association challenge of the annual subsidies given to Ottawa, Edmonton and Calgary to help offset the costs of operating teams in small Canadian markets.

The NHLPA has filed a complaint against the league with the National Labor Relations Board, saying that one of the criteria for those three teams to qualify for assistance is based on having a payroll that is among the league's lowest. The NHLPA contends that holds down player salaries on those clubs.

Overall, Bettman contends the league is in good shape. Revenue streams are up with the construction of five new arenas and a new television deal with ABC and ESPN that starts with the 1999–2000 season. There is labor peace until 2004 and the league is still trying to work out details on whether or not to send players to the 2002 Olympic Games in Salt Lake City.

Still, problems remain. Pittsburgh and its $120 million debt are a major problem. The NHL is negotiating with Nassau County politicians in an attempt to construct a new facility for the Islanders. The Phoenix Coyotes, the league's surprise success story this season on the ice, are looking to build a new facility in Scottsdale.

The Canadian dollar sits at 65 cents when measured against the U.S. dollar and some of the "newer" expansion cities like Tampa are having problems filling seats. The cost of a ticket to a game has gone through the roof in most cities.

"We think we can resolve the building situation (on Long Island), because if you look at the last five years, I think there are 15 new buildings and by the time the wave of buildings that are currently on line are completed, there will be less than a handful of teams in older buildings," said Bettman.

"The Islanders will be in one of the oldest buildings with one of the worst leases, and in order for them to be competitive and viable, they need a new building. We are working very hard with the county and Islander ownership to resolve that issue. I am hopefully optimistic that the efforts we are engaged in are going to be productive."

Pittsburgh is a thorny problem. A bankruptcy judge has allowed the team to borrow $20 million from a French bank to allow the club to meet expenses and player payroll for the rest of the 1998–99 season. The Penguins were so strapped for cash that they used money picked up from the Rangers in a trade to issue checks to players.

"This (the Penguins) is a club that accumulated too much debt. It plays in one of the oldest buildings with one of the worst leases and we are trying to clean it up," said Bettman. "We have had a number of franchises that we have worked with over the last few years to improve and get stronger. This one needed that type of help and only the protection of Chapter 11 could afford it. We will have to work our way through this."

Bob Goodenow, the Executive Director of the NHL Players' Association, is keeping a keen eye on the Pittsburgh situation. There are 24 association members who are assured of receiving their money this season, but there are former Penguins players on the bankruptcy list waiting for back pay, including Mario Lemieux.

"Any time a team has a financial situation which forces them to take steps into bankruptcy, it is a serious problem," said Goodenow. "The Pittsburgh situation has been compounded over the years because of their situation with the building. There seems to be a lot of turmoil with the business aspects of the franchise.

"Yes, it is a problem. But I think it is a good hockey city and I know the team is working hard and has a nice product on the ice. Hopefully, it will work itself out."

The league would like to remain in Pittsburgh. Ironically, the Penguins declared bankruptcy once before, on June 13, 1975, and were sold about a month later to local interests who prevented the team from moving to Seattle.

A Canadian parliament commission has suggested tax breaks for NHL teams, something that Bettman would welcome. However, the Mills Commission Report is just that, a report.

"When we went to the Mills Commission, it was with the hope that there would be a recognition that beyond being Canada's national pastime, we made significant economic contributions," Bettman said. "We have made a billion dollars in private infrastructure investment, be it over $400 million a year in taxes, be it 11–12,000 jobs from our teams in their arenas.

"We said, 'If you recognize that we are an important economic engine, we would like you to then consider whether or not we are being fairly treated.' There area a number of industries in Canada where the government has recognized that in order to effectively complete outside of Canada things had to be done."

Bettman said he never asked for a subsidy for the Canadian teams, rather fair treatment. He illustrated his point by using the Montreal Canadiens as an example.

"The Canadiens built the Molson Centre with private funds. It was the biggest construction in downtown Montreal in the last ten years," he said. "The end result was an $11 million real estate tax bill which is three times what the United States teams (21) pay collectively.

"Ottawa is another example. Their tax bills are more than the U.S. teams collectively. They also had to have their own exit ramp to the arena from the Trans-Canada Highway. That does not normally happen. Normally, the infrastructure support is provided by the local government.

"When you look at that kind of treatment, you ask, 'Is that fair? Is that enabling us to have our teams in Canada be competitive?' We are looking for a recognition of those issues."

One problem that will not go away is the difference between the value of the Canadian and American dollar.

"That also hurts and that's something we discussed because our teams compete in U.S. dollars for playing talent," Bettman said. "But there are a number of industries in Canada that make it very appealing for the Canadian dollar to be low relative to the U.S. dollar. This is an industry where we are on the flipside of that."

Toronto's associate GM, Mike Smith, thinks the Mills Commission may provide the impetus that will get "various levels of government thinking more aggressively in supporting NHL hockey." Smith said he hopes that government officials will realize Canadian teams need tax breaks.

The NHL is trying to negotiate a deal with the International Olympic Committee for 2002 participation of its players and receive assurance from NBC that hockey will be prominently covered in prime time in Salt Lake City. NBC has not given the league that assurance as of yet and the decision of the players on competing in the next Olympics has also not come.

"The International Hockey agreement is really nowhere right now. Our understanding (of player participation) ends with the World Championship of 1999," Goodenow explained. "Going beyond that, our previous agreement which covered the World Cup, the World Championships and the Olympics is up for discussion.

"There are a whole host of issues and points to be dealt with and they have to be taken care of within the next six to 12 months."

Vancouver's Pavel Bure is sitting out and players such as New York's Zigmund Palffy and Colorado's Sandis Ozolinsh are looking for new deals and holding out.

"I don't think anyone likes it when top players are not playing. When we went through our negotiations, I understood that situations (holdouts) like this do, in fact, occur," Goodenow said. "It's a fact of life now how contracts are negotiated. It's unfortunate, but those matters have a way of getting themselves resolved at some point of time."

Does the NHL's present labor agreement work?

"I am sure that people on the management side are satisfied with some areas more than others. And I think that's true on our side," Goodenow said. "On the context that neither side is happy with all areas, maybe it's a deal that works. But it's hard to tell in a short time span."

The NHL of the 21st century will feature 30 teams and a new television contract. Atlanta enters the league in 1999 followed by St. Paul, Minnesota and Columbus, Ohio in 2000. So far, Bettman is pleased with those franchises from the business viewpoint. "They are doing very well. They are converting their season tickets lists into commitments and I think they are all going to get off to great starts," he said. "Atlanta is still selling their season tickets, but I think they do have the bulk of them sold and the building is under construction. We are expecting only good things from the three remaining expansion cities."

With the four latest expansion teams, the shifting of two Canadian teams into Phoenix and Denver, and expansion into Florida and California, the NHL's U.S. "footprint" is radically different from a decade ago.

"If you go back to 1990, we were in 11 U.S. markets and that includes multiple teams in New York. When we get done with expansion, we will be over 20," Bettman said. "That makes us more competitive with the other guys (baseball, football and basketball) who are in between 25 and 30 markets."

"Disney has been involved with us through the Mighty Ducks, ESPN and ESPN2. We think the opportunity to cross promote between ABC, ESPN and ESPN2 will help," added Bettman, referring to the new TV contract. FOX has done a really good job for us, but as we move forward, we are looking forward to the ABC opportunity."

Storm Clouds Threaten Baseball's 'Recovery'
Street & Smith's Sportsbusiness Journal, August 1998

Sportswriters are boasting that baseball is back, as compelling as ever, and that New York has become the baseball capital of the world. But how strong, really, is the baseball recovery from the 1994 strike, World Series cancellation and the late start of the 1995 season?

For all the on-field accomplishments so far, all the Mark McGwire home runs, the David Wells perfect game and the New York Yankees' remarkable start, there are storm clouds brewing. A good number of clubs are not even pretending to compete for a championship. That list starts with Florida and includes Pittsburgh, Montreal, Cincinnati and Oakland.

Television ratings are not terribly strong, although merchandising sales are supposed to be up. Interleague play has met with indifference, and the voting public seems no longer in the mood to build taxpayer-assisted stadiums for baseball teams.

The Florida Marlins traded off virtually all of their high-priced players; the 1997 World Championship resembles a Class AA or AAA team instead of a defending titlist.

In recent weeks, two teams indicated they may be relocating shortly. Another, the Yankees of George Steinbrenner, threatened to move to New Jersey if New York City asks voters whether they want to build a new stadium.

The owners of the Athletics have until Friday to decide whether they will remain in Oakland or begin the process of selling or moving the team.

The Montreal Expos ownership has decided to stay in the city through the 1999 season; however, the team will know by Sept. 30 of this year whether it can proceed with plans to build a new stadium. If the Expos fail to sell enough luxury boxes/personal seat licenses, the club will be sold and moved.

Expo fans might not notice the difference between a major league or a minor league team anyway, as most of Montreal's good players have been sold off.

The Minnesota Twins situation remains murky. Voters in Greensboro, N.C., and its surrounding area, in May overwhelmingly rejected a proposal to build a stadium for the Twins in Minneapolis, and the team is for sale.

Meanwhile, the big-market teams like the Yankees, New York Mets and Los Angeles Dodgers are swinging big trades or spending big money to fortify rosters, creating a baseball society of select aristocrats at one end and a good number of ne'er-do-wells at the other end, with very few teams in the middle.

Before the 1994 strike, there was a competitive balance and teams did not have to have the highest payrolls in the game to go to the playoffs. That has changed, as teams with big television contracts, a good number of luxury boxes and sweetheart leases with cities control the game.

Without meaningful revenue sharing, more mismatches like the recent $70 million-or-more payroll Yankees against the $9 million-payroll Expos will become more commonplace and fan interest will subside in the cities that cannot compete. It would be healthy for baseball if Kansas City could compete with Los Angeles, or Cincinnati with New York, but it is not happening.

The recovery that sportswriters are boasting about may very well be illusory if the owners cannot agree on a revenue-sharing plan that will close the discrepancy between the haves and have-nots. After all, what is the compelling reason to see the Expos or Marlins with a bunch of minor leaguers in their lineups play the Yankees? Even if New York is the center of the baseball world.

Is Bush a Fiscal Conservative or Liberal Spender?
Houston Business Journal, 2000

Does Texas Governor and Republican presidential front-runner George W. Bush believe in his party's position of smaller government by the reduction of agencies and a reduction of taxes? One of the planks of Bush's 2000 platform is a call for smaller government and a tax cut. But when it comes to pro sports, Bush does not exactly practice what he preaches.

Bush, whose family has been in the business of government for three generations—his grandfather Prescott was a U.S. senator from Connecticut, his father George was president from 1989 to 1993 and had a long career in big government including a stint as CIA director, and his brother Jeb is Florida governor—owned a piece of the Texas Rangers between 1989 and 1994. He put the club in a trust after being elected governor of Texas and finally sold the team to Thomas O. Hicks in 1998.

Hicks was a big-pockets contributor to the Bush gubernatorial campaigns.

In 1989, Bush invested some $600,000 to control 2 percent interest in the Rangers. The ownership group went to Arlington Mayor Richard Greene in 1990 and told Greene a new stadium was needed or the team would move, possibly to St. Petersburg.

Arlington residents eventually passed a referendum that raised the local sales tax by 0.5 percent to fund up to 70 percent of the cost of the stadium. The Ballpark in Arlington opened in 1994. Bush and his partners not only had a new park, but they controlled 270 acres of land surrounding the stadium—land which they got from Arlington through eminent domain. The stadium and the 270 acres of land cost $196 million, with about $135 million coming from the sales tax. Bush sold the team and the rights to land around the park in 1998 and received $14 million for his share. The total purchase price was $250 million for the team, the ballpark—which was built by Arlington residents—and the land.

Businessmen are entitled to profits and can use whatever legal means to forward a business. But Bush's call for fiscal responsibility, tax cuts and small government by having fewer government agencies smacks of hypocrisy. His wheeling and dealing in sports was because of government largesse.

In 1997, the Texas Legislature was faced with numerous stadium and arena problems in Houston and Dallas. Astros owner Drayton McLane told Houston officials that he was going to follow the lead of Oilers owner K. S. "Bud" Adams and move from Houston without a new stadium. Hicks, owner of the NHL Stars, and the Dallas Mavericks were looking for a new arena.

The Legislature put together a big government package for sports and other cultural projects. Local municipalities could raise hotel/motel occupancy and car rental taxes by as much as 2 percent to fund arenas, stadiums, museums, libraries, convention centers, concert halls and other venues.

Gov. Bush signed the bill into law while he still owned the Texas Rangers. The law ensured government involvement in private enterprise and would raise taxes if voters approved referendums.

The new law helped Hicks immediately, and Dallas voters passed legislation to build a new arena. McLane got his new stadium in Houston, and the NFL will be getting a stadium for the new Houston expansion team. Voters in San Antonio/Bexar County approved raising hotel and motel tax rates along with car rental taxes for a new indoor arena for the Spurs.

Voters turned down a new basketball arena in Houston, but arena proponents plan to raise the question again in 2000 as Houston Rockets owner Leslie Alexander's lease winds down at Compaq Center.

Alexander can become a free agent in 2003.

Bush also approved legislation in 1999 that paves the way for Houston and Dallas to seek the 2012 Summer Olympic Games. In another government move, the Texas Legislature passed a bill allowing either city to guarantee its bid with sales tax revenue generated from Olympic-related items.

Houston and Dallas voters would have to approve of the idea of hosting the Olympics and allow the tax. The sales tax would meet the U.S. Olympic Committee requirement that the host city's state would pick up the costs of Olympic-related overruns.

The Houston 2012 Foundation would like to get the referendum before voters in November when presumably the Texas governor is the Republican candidate for president.

So is George W. Bush a fiscal conservative who wants to cut back on "big government" and government spending? Or is George W. Bush a liberal spender who endorses government help in private enterprises like sports?

It's a question Bush should answer.

Let's Field a Third Major League Ball Club

Newsday, New York City Edition, December 5, 2001

LET ME GET this straight. There is an international business based in New York that claims to have lost $500 million in the past calendar year and that 25 out of its 30 outlets are money losers. It contends that the outlook is so bleak that two of its franchises need to be shuttered immediately. Yet, this company has just given its CEO a three-year contract extension as a reward for doing a good job, and one of its division leaders is ready to give an employee a reported seven-year, $120-million contract.

Welcome to the world of Major League Baseball. In this often confusing world, Commissioner Bud Selig, the one-time owner of the Milwaukee Brewers (his daughter now owns the business), will go to Congress tomorrow and, with a straight face, ask a House panel to embrace the idea of eliminating two teams for the betterment of the product.

Getting rid of two teams reduces the industry's losses, which means that the owners would split national revenues 28 ways instead of 30. But it is not the national revenues that causes the gap between big- and small-market teams. It's local TV revenue.

So why is Selig in front of Congress pleading poverty? Baseball has an anti-trust exemption. It also lives off the public, considering how many of its ballparks have been built with taxpayers' money.

The House Judiciary Committee is holding hearings to make sure Major League Baseball tows the line and keeps its 30 franchises going. Congress wouldn't fret too much about eliminating the Montreal Expos but folding the Minnesota Twins does present a problem.

Minnesota Sens. Mark Dayton and Paul Wellstone have said they want to hold Senate hearings on baseball's anti-trust exemption. They may want to punish Major League Baseball for daring to junk Minnesota by stripping the industry's protection in retaliation for contraction. But why not really put a scare into the Lords of Baseball by threatening to dismantle the 30-team cartel? All they have to do is follow the breakup of AT&T. Major League Baseball has been a monopoly since the Supreme Court granted it an anti-trust exemption in 1922. Because of the major leagues' power, New York doesn't have three major league teams today. New legislation could remedy that. After the Dodgers and Giants announced their move to the West Coast in 1957, the National League would not allow teams from Cincinnati or Pittsburgh to move to New York.

In fact, Major League Baseball had no intention to return National League baseball to New York until it was pushed by the formation of the Continental League in the late '50s. That league never got off the ground. The threat of competition, however, forced the National League to recognize that it had to offer New York baseball fans a new team.

A third New York team would have what it needs to be successful: government support; lucrative local TV rights (the Madison Square Garden network needs summer programming since it lost the Yanks); a huge corporate base and thousands of fans. The recent stunning success of the short-season minor league Brooklyn Cyclones and the Staten Island Yankees is enough evidence that the city has an appetite for more baseball. Considering the potential revenue, it would be better to be the third most popular baseball team in New York than to be the only baseball team in towns such as Kansas City or St. Petersburg.

There have been reports that Montreal Expos owner Jeffrey Loria would like to relocate his team to our area, but he can't because existing baseball rules limit the New York territory to George Steinbrenner and Fred Wilpon and Nelson Doubleday. Loria, a native New Yorker, is a Manhattan art dealer. Moving the Expos to New York makes sense for baseball, for New York and for him. Adding a third Major League team would certainly mean cutting into the Yankees' and Mets' revenues but they could afford it. And besides, it would level the playing field by bringing the finances of the Yankees and the Mets closer to the more cash-strapped teams. And it's doable. The Yankees shared Shea Stadium with the Mets in 1974 and 1975. Both the Yanks and the Mets would be hard-pressed to say no to a business willing to pay money to use a city-owned facility.

Major League Baseball officials and those connected to the Yankees and Mets may argue that having three big league teams in New York would saturate us with baseball. But the National Hockey League has the Devils, the Rangers and the Islanders, three New

York-area teams that coexist in the market with heated rivalries. There have been nights when all three played at the same time before sold-out crowds. Congress should take a major step and strip Major League Baseball of its anti-trust protection. Then, New York can get its third team and possibly recreate the Golden Age of Baseball of the late 1940s and '50s, when all three city teams were regulars in the World Series.

Welcome to the Unreal World of N.Y. Baseball

Newsday, New York City Edition, June 14, 2002

There will not be any Kmart Blue Light Specials as the 2002 Subway Series gets under way tonight at Shea. This is prime New York sirloin. Only when the Islanders and Rangers play one another are the fans more intense. The audience will be tightly wound anticipating a Roger Clemens-Mike Piazza showdown possible on Saturday. We may then find out whether the Rocket has been hiding behind the designated hitter rule all these years.

Baseball in the Big Apple goes back nearly 160 years. The Giants literally threw the Yankees out of the Polo Grounds in the 1920s. Brooklyn Dodgers fans had a dislike for the New York Giants fans —and their players—and vice versa. Bobby Thomson's home run off Ralph Branca in the 1951 National League playoff is still baseball's top moment as Russ Hodges repeated the mantra, "The Giants win the pennant! The Giants win the pennant! The Giants win the pennant!" The Brooklyn-born Joe Torre grew up as a Giants fan, Mets manager Bobby Valentine's father-in-law is Branca. Valentine played for Torre when the Yankee skipper piloted the Mets in the late 1970s.

Both the Giants and the Dodgers fans had something in common: their hatred of the Yankees, who almost always beat their teams. Those Giants and Dodgers fans eventually became Mets fans, and even though 45 years have passed since the Dodgers and Giants called New York City home, not much has changed. Major League Baseball blew a tremendous opportunity to reconnect with its roots by not having the sense to schedule the Dodgers in Yankee Stadium earlier this week after the Yankees hosted the Giants.

While this weekend's games at Shea will draw more than 150,000 paying customers, dominate the radio sports talk shows, fill newspaper space and glue TV viewers to the screen, it's not the most important story going around baseball. And, in that sense, New Yorkers are isolated from the real world of baseball. A world where Baseball Commissioner Bud Selig contends that six to eight teams are on the verge of going out of business, and 18 of its 30 franchises have been considered candidates for contraction. A world where baseball officials admit that they are using Kmart as a business role model.

In April, Major League Baseball's chief operating officer, Bob Dupuy, told the *Washington Post*, "One thing the commissioner felt he could do unilaterally was to close plants. Kmart filed for bankruptcy and closed, what 280 out of 2,000—not because they wanted to close 280 stores, but to let 2,000 other stores survive. That's essentially the theory behind contraction."

In this baseball world, small-market franchises can only look up to the Yankees (and even the Mets) and give them their best players in exchange for cash and prospects because they can't afford to play at the same level as New York's franchises.

Even if baseball lopped off two teams, the small markets still can't compete with George Steinbrenner, the Yankees, the YES Network, WCBS-TV, the New York corporate community and the spending power of Yankees fans. Nor can small markets keep up with Fred Wilpon, Nelson Doubleday, the Mets, the Madison Square Garden Network/FOX Sports Net and WPIX, just to name a few.

Over the years, the Yankees have used other major league teams as sort of a farm system. In the 1950s, Kansas City developed such players as Clete Boyer and Roger Maris and eventually traded them over to the Yankees for players and cash. In the 1970s, the Yankees sent players and cash to the Cleveland Indians and the Chicago White Sox for Graig Nettles and Bucky Dent and signed free agents such as Catfish Hunter and Reggie Jackson. This year, the Yankees spent $120 million for Jason Giambi. The Pinstripes, from Col. Jacob Ruppert to Steinbrenner, always had money to buy players for the House That Babe Built.

Sure, it would be healthy for baseball if small markets could compete with the Yankees. (It would be healthier mentally for Mets fans if the Mets could compete with the Yanks.) But baseball has never had competitive balance. It doesn't matter to the New York fans anyway. They want their teams to meet in October and hope this weekend's confrontations are just a dress rehearsal for the Fall Classic. Let the small market teams hold their own Blue Light Special promotion with Selig or Dupuy throwing out the first ball. The intense rivalry of the Subway Series is the way baseball ought to be.

Baseball Fans Put Up with So Much Drama
The Cleveland Plain-Dealer, July 19, 2002

Real baseball fans don't deserve what they are getting: contraction, congressional hearings, steroids, lawsuits, All-Star Game ties, accusations of racketeering and, of course, the possibility of a strike. All of this gets in the way of what baseball fans want: the game.

Indians fans shouldn't be hearing Larry Dolan blasting New York Yankees owner and Cleveland native George Steinbrenner for contributing to baseball's financial problems.

Baseball fans were better off when Bud Selig was called "Jerry Lewis" by his Milwaukee players because of his resemblance to the nutty professor character. Now the former 14 Montreal Expos partners are citing RICO laws and accusing Selig and former Expos owner Jeffrey Loria of racketeering in taking their share of the Expos away. People think of Selig as a used-car salesman, not Tony Soprano. But baseball could be on trial defending itself against wire and mail fraud charges.

Major League Baseball apparently doesn't care that it has violated its trust with its fans, partners, sponsors and advertisers. The integrity of the 2002 season was compromised two days after one of the most exciting World Series ever when Commissioner Bud Selig announced that two franchises needed to be eliminated. In addition, the owners and players started the season without a collective bargaining agreement.

Major League Baseball has damaged the Montreal franchise beyond repair for one-time Expo fans. Minnesota fought to keep the Twins. A good number of clubs are not even pretending to compete for a championship, including the Indians.

According to Major League Baseball, 18 of its 30 franchises were considered candidates for contraction. While Barry Bonds was slugging home runs during the first week of the season, baseball's lawyers in Minneapolis were arguing that they could fold the Twins. And the reason baseball wants contraction? They want to be just like Kmart. Yes, Kmart—the retailer that is in bankruptcy.

President and Chief Operating Officer Bob DuPuy told the *Washington Post*, "One thing the commissioner felt he could do unilaterally was to close plants. Kmart filed for bankruptcy and closed—what, 280 out of 2,000?—not because they wanted to close 280 stores, but to let 2,000 other stores survive. That's essentially the theory behind contraction."

So baseball was willing to sacrifice the Expos and Twins to make sure the Yankees stayed in business. How nice.

Why would people want to buy into the industry by purchasing tickets, club seats, luxury boxes and watching games on TV? Why are there more corporate partners pumping in money than ever before?

It must be the game itself.

Remarkably, the baseball fan has shown resiliency despite baseball's best efforts to present itself in the worst economic light. More money than ever is flowing into baseball from TV, advertisers, partnerships and fans. This despite Minnesota's going to court to force Major League Baseball to honor its lease with the Minneapolis Metrodome in 2002. This despite the cable TV battle of New York between Cablevision and Steinbrenner. This despite *Forbes* magazine accusing baseball of doctoring the books and claiming that the industry was profitable in 2001, while Selig says baseball lost hundreds of millions of dollars.

It seems to be a case of believability. It reminds me of Chico Marx asking, "Who are you gonna believe: your eyes or me?"

The grand recovery of Major League Baseball that Selig has been touting since the 1994–95 labor strife has been nothing more than an illusion, because the owners have not come up with a revenue-sharing plan that would close the discrepancy between the "haves" (the Yankees and the Mets) and the "have-nots" (Pittsburgh, Montreal, Tampa Bay and Kansas City).

Baseball used to be the national pastime. It is quickly becoming past-its-time. And that's too bad for real baseball fans, who have no say in its future and want to just watch the game.

George, at Least, Knows How to Win This Game
Newsday, New York Edition, August 7, 2002

My friend Don Chevrier, the voice of Olympic Curling and long-time Toronto Blue Jays announcer, recently told me that he's all in favor of baseball contraction, as long as baseball eliminates George Steinbrenner and the New York Mets. That would, according to Chevrier with his tongue firmly planted in his cheek, solve all of baseball's financial woes.

Well, Chevy may have been trying to make light of the state of baseball but Cleveland Indians owner Lawrence Dolan, the brother of Cablevision Chairman Charles Dolan and a major Cablevision stockholder, was more blunt.

"George is a large part of our problem," Dolan said in early July after Baseball Commissioner Bud Selig allowed owners to discuss baseball's labor negotiations. "George is not spending George's money. George is spending revenue money the rest of us don't have."

Larry Dolan is correct. Steinbrenner isn't spending Steinbrenner's money.

He is spending our cable TV money that he is collecting from the YES Network—well, from some of us, anyway, since Charles Dolan isn't putting the new Yankee network on his cable system.

George Steinbrenner and Yankee fans shouldn't be pushed around by the other Major League Baseball owners. If there is a players' strike, it will be because the other owners want to get back at Steinbrenner. Most of the other owners are convinced that the only way to beat the Yankees is to take Steinbrenner's money and give it to needy teams.

Other teams, notably the Orioles, have spent huge sums of money on players and haven't been successful. The Yankees not only have money, but may also have the smartest talent evaluators in baseball.

Yet, too many of the other owners discount the Yankees' front-office intelligence. They think Steinbrenner simply gets too many dollars from his local cable-TV deal and that gives him an unfair advantage in recruiting players. Steinbrenner's spending is ruining baseball's competitive balance, they contend.

The other owners' revenue-sharing plan should make the New York-area cable subscribers, and Steinbrenner, irate. I, along with many others, am already spending money for a service I don't want, the YES Network. I was forced to take YES because I want to watch cable TV. Because of that, I should be entitled, along with my fellow New York subscribers, to have a say. Our money better stay here.

I don't want the Walt Disney Company in Anaheim or Carl Pohlad in Minnesota or David Glass in Kansas City or the Selig family in Milwaukee to get one thin dime of our contribution to the Yankees' revenue stream. At least, Steinbrenner is playing by Major League Baseball's rules.

Baseball should have come up with a way of sharing media money equitably seven decades ago when radio stations began bidding for broadcasting rights. The sport should have figured out a mechanism of dealing with television monies in the 1950s, when the Yankees started getting more TV money than the other teams.

Baseball should have seen that the cable industry would emerge as the dominant media player in the late 1970s. But the owners have never been visionaries.

If a team can't make it financially, let them fold. Restaurants, department stores and other businesses close up shop. The Tampa Bay Devil Rays and the Montreal Expos can do the same. Why should New York money prop up those teams?

But there is an alternative to the owners' huge revenue-sharing scheme, which could save teams from contraction. Congress should re-regulate the cable industry and give us subscribers the right to choose what channels we want and let us know how much we are being charged per channel.

Because sports has a relatively small audience of serious fans, the buy rates for cable TV sports would drastically fall if sports channels were offered a la carte. Suddenly, enormous sums of cash wouldn't be there, and that would level the playing field because sports franchises would just get money from sports fans. It's a fairer system.

But, until Congress acts, all of us have to pay for sports on cable. And, as long as we have to pay, we shouldn't let baseball owners punish Steinbrenner, Yankee fans and New Yorkers. They want to take our cable TV money away from our team to prevent it from signing the top-of-the-line players and, instead, give those dollars to needy teams so they can end their money woes.

I say, "fuhgeddaboudit." Let's keep our money in New York.

Bush Can't Help in Baseball Talks

NBCSports.com, August 28, 2002

I was watching CNN the other night and there came the tease, "Can Bush Solve Baseball Problems?" I started thinking, Bush can't convince America's allies to get involved in an action against Sadaam Hussein, nor has he been able to lift the stock market or turn around the sagging economy.

Now it's a possible baseball strike.

But for baseball fans, Bush represents a ray of hope. And it's not only CNN asking if Bush can intercede and produce results. Sportswriters are wondering if Bush can do something to stop a strike.

The answer is no. Bush may be furious that the players walk but here's the problem: George W. Bush once owned the Texas Rangers and that presents a major obstacle.

Bush was one of those owners who have whined since 1881 that rising player salaries will ruin baseball. He also benefited greatly from baseball and its unique status as a sport.

In 1922, Supreme Court Chief Justice Oliver Wendell Holmes in a landmark decision granting Major League Baseball an anti-trust exemption said baseball was a sport. He was wrong. Baseball is a business.

President Bush, you see, was part of the problem in 1990 and 1994. In fact fans hoping that Bush will use the bully pulpit of the Oval Office to force a settlement better ask some questions about the President's Ranger past before thinking of asking him to get involved.

Bush spent $600,000 to buy a piece of the Rangers in 1989 after selling his shares in Harken Energy. There is still a cloud hanging over that transaction. Bush, who was the team's general managing partner, threatened to move the Rangers to St. Petersburg, Florida, unless Arlington, Texas, gave the group a taxpayer's funded stadium.

Arlington eventually capitulated and approved a sales tax hike for a stadium and got the land for the stadium by eminent domain.

What was Bush's role in the 1992 coup d'état, which saw Commissioner Fay Vincent fired? Bush wanted to be the commissioner. What was Bush's role in the 1994 baseball strike, a strike that was ended by Federal Judge Sonia Sotomayer who found the baseball owners had not bargained in good faith?

Incidentally, Judge Sotomayer was appointed to the bench by Bush's father.

What was Bush's role with the Rangers while he was Texas governor and how involved was he in selling the club to Tom Hicks in 1998? Bush walked away with a $13.4 million profit.

Bush would need to answer those questions before anyone would consider getting him aboard. So, it is unlikely Bush would be accepted as an honest broker by the players association.

So the fans shouldn't count on White House intervention.

As Bush showed, owners need local mayors, governors, city councils and state legislatures to buy into the notion that they need new stadiums to survive and more often than not the politicians have come up with stadiums built on the public dime.

Owners need corporate support to buy the big-ticket items, luxury boxes and club seating. Incidentally, those seats quickly become tax write offs for corporations and you know those big salaries that the owners are paying players? Well, the owners can depreciate the contracts much like you can depreciate a car on your tax return.

During the Bush years as Ranger owner from 1989–98, baseball became a cable TV show and elitist entertainment. Once upon a time, baseball didn't segregate its fans. The fabulously rich person could sit next to someone who was struggling to eke out a living. Now the rich person sits in a box, separated from the everyday rift raft.

The only place where baseball fans are equal is in front of the cable TV set. All 86.5 million-cable subscribers pay pretty much the same rate for games on basic cable and are forced to take sports networks as part of their cable package because Congress and the FCC deregulated the cable industry.

So the fans shouldn't count on Congressional intervention either. Congress by not removing baseball's anti-trust exemption and deregulating cable also contributed to the baseball labor mess.

Fans may whine about never returning to watch Major League Baseball if the players strike on August 30. But both the owners and players know this; as long as there is government support, a strong local cable contract and corporate interest, baseball is set. That's why neither Bush nor Congress could be honest brokers in the baseball dispute.

And that's the sad truth for die-hard fans.

A Losing Proposition
Baltimore Sun, December 8, 2002

Peter Angelos got an early Christmas present from his 28 fellow owners. The Lords of Baseball have decided that San Juan, Puerto Rico, is a better place to stage some of the Montreal Expos "home" games than Washington, D.C., next year.

But if Mr. Angelos thinks he has avoided getting competition in his back yard, he may be in for a surprise. Baseball could move the Expos to Washington in time for the 2004 season, and that's not only bad news for him but also for potential Washington fans because of how major-league sports is structured.

It's all about money. Big money from government, cable TV and corporations.

Sometime during 2003, Major League Baseball, which owns the Montreal Expos, will put the team up for sale. The prevailing wisdom is that baseball will accept a bid from a Washington and/or a Northern Virginia group of businessmen backed by government officials, cable TV executives and corporate leaders who will promise baseball a new taxpayer-supported stadium and an open checkbook.

The Expos will then relocate within an hour of Baltimore. But there is no need for Orioles fans to worry. It won't hurt the O's bottom line that much.

Yeah, right.

Mr. Angelos was absolutely correct when he said, "You wouldn't put another team in the same market with Boston, or in the same market with St. Louis, or in the same market with Minnesota. Why, then, 30 miles from Camden Yards?"

But he should be worried. He knows a successful franchise needs four ingredients: government support, a large cable TV contract, corporate support and, last and least, fan support.

Mr. Angelos has government support; after all, Maryland did build Camden Yards for the Orioles. At the moment, he has corporate support, because companies are buying his luxury boxes and club seating. And he controls his cable TV product on Comcast's regional sports network.

But should the Expos move to Washington, Mr. Angelos' revenue sources will be hurt—and prospects for the transplanted Washington team won't be that much better than the previous two Washington baseball franchises, which moved in 1960 and 1971.

The Orioles' large market will shrink in a hurry. Officially, its "territory" will consist of just Baltimore and six surrounding counties. The TV market figures to be downsized as well.

As the area's only current baseball franchise, the Orioles get an enormous amount of money from cable TV. The team has lined up some 4.2 million households in Maryland, Virginia, Delaware, Washington and parts of West Virginia and Pennsylvania that can receive Oriole baseball.

If Washington were to get a team, the Orioles would lose a significant number of households in the capital region because Major League Baseball would give the transplanted team cable rights in Washington and parts of Virginia that are now part of the Orioles' cable network.

Additionally, the Orioles could not televise games on broadcast Washington TV or market in Washington. That would cost Mr. Angelos and the Orioles millions of dollars annually and depress Washington's potential TV earnings.

Moreover, if Robert Johnson, the founder of Black Entertainment Television, ends up with the Washington franchise, he wants to start his own cable network to bring in much-needed revenues.

Will Comcast allow a Johnson/Washington sports cable network on its systems throughout the mid-Atlantic to compete with the Comcast regional sports network? It's universally known that the federal government-allowed cable monopoly doesn't take kindly to competition.

The Orioles are also battling for corporate dollars with the Ravens, Redskins, Wizards, Capitals, Mystics, D.C. United, University of Maryland and other colleges and a number of minor-league teams. The Orioles and a Washington team would go after the same clients, and there are just so many companies that are interested in sports in the area. This would also cost the Orioles millions of dollars annually and hurt Washington's corporate support.

Without those revenue streams, teams become non-competitive and perennial losers, like baseball Commissioner Bud Selig's Milwaukee Brewers.

The Orioles and Senators didn't work between 1954 and 1971 when the state and local governments weren't partners with teams and cable TV was nothing more than someone running a wire up a mountain. The Orioles and Expos won't work in 2004, either.

Mets' New Pricing System Looks Like Fool's Gold

Newsday, New York City Edition, December 27, 2002

In keeping with the spirit of the holiday season, it's time for baseball fans to give something back to their team, that is, if they want to pay for advance tickets. So here's a question for Mets ticket buyers: Will you be going for the Gold, the Silver or the Bronze, and will you be hoping to get some value for your baseball bucks? I'm not talking about the 2012 Summer Olympics here, I'm talking about seeing Art Howe's Mets in 2003— minus Edgardo Alfonso, Rey Ordonez, and a stellar outfield. The team seems to be a work in progress.

Both the Mets and the Yankees have raised their ticket prices. For the Yankees, it's a $2-to-$10-dollar price hike but Boss George Steinbrenner is also giving something back to his fans. On eight selected days, the Yankees are selling about 26,000 upper-deck tickets for $5. But this year you need a calculator and a calendar to figure out how much to pay for Mets tickets.

The Mets have introduced four ticket packages: "Gold" for teams like the Yankees, the Mariners, the Giants, the Cardinals, the Braves, and for special events like Opening Day against the Cubs and Fireworks Night in July against the Expos. The "Silver" plan is a weekend deal, and you get the Braves at a slightly cheaper rate than the "Gold" plan. The "Bronze" plan freezes prices at 2002 levels and offers some weekend dates against lesser lights like the Expos and the Padres. The "Value" plan gives you cold-weather games or small-market teams like the Pirates and the Brewers.

Here's a tip: If it's cold and not the weekend and the Mets aren't playing Derek Jeter, Barry Bonds or Chipper Jones, you are probably getting a break on the cost of a ticket. But don't count on it.

Mets tickets will be available for as low as $8 for cheapskates dying to see the Phillies and as high as $53 for those who can afford to see the Bronx Bombers.

Welcome to baseball's new world of variable ticket pricing. The Mets are merely following the lead of the Colorado Rockies, the Cardinals, the Giants and the Indians, and joining the Chicago

Cubs and the World Champion Anaheim Angels in what might be considered legal scalping.

Something bothers me about the owners' latest scheme to show the general public that they really do have their fans' best interests at heart. Why did the owners collude in trying to separate George Steinbrenner and his cable TV money (they succeeded by getting revenue sharing) and, like the Rockies and the Mets, charge fans more money to see his Yankees in person?

It seems the Yankees play a purpose for Major League Baseball owners. They blame Steinbrenner for ruining baseball's economic structure, yet jack up the prices for the fans when the Yankees come to town.

Meanwhile, these ticket-pricing changes come after baseball announced it was forming a task force to try to figure out why the game has become America's Past-its-Time. Baseball's television ratings have been on a steady decline since the 1970s. The 2002 World Series match up between the Anaheim Angels and the San Francisco Giants was the least-watched seven-game series in recent television history—despite having home-run king Barry Bonds on the roster.

Baseball Commissioner Bud Selig wants to know what to do to improve the game, how to increase attendance and raise ratings. He hasn't invited me to be part of his think tank, but I will give him some free advice anyway. Steinbrenner is making some 220,000 tickets available at $5 each. That is a major step in the right direction. More teams should reduce ticket prices and offer more games on local free TV instead of depending exclusively on cable to deliver the product. They should reinstitute senior citizens' day so a grandparent who wants to be with his or her grandchild can afford to spend a summer's day at the ballpark. Let's slash parking costs and concession prices on special days. And why not bring back the G.O. card— the general organization card given to New York City public school students in the good old days that got them discounts at sports venues and some local businesses?

The cost of a ticket is not the starting point for a fan. Getting to a game costs money. New Jersey Mets fans who drive have to shell out $13 in tolls; Long Island Yankee fans have to pay $7 in tolls. Add that to the high cost of parking.

The 7 p.m. first pitch doesn't help fans, either, because it cuts out time for dinner after work and forces people to buy expensive ballpark food or go hungry. Stadium paraphernalia and team merchandise cost money, too, as parents know all too well.

The trend is clear. Baseball has priced out the average family. Once the working class was the backbone of the sports economic system. It's not anymore.

Owners have forgotten that fans' dollars support the product. Fans bring the stadiums to life. They shouldn't have to go for the gold to see a game.

Beyond New York, Baseball Season Looks Dim
Newsday, New York City Edition, March 27, 2003

As I was leaving town the other day, I made sure I brought along my old, battered copy of Jim Bouton's "Ball Four" to read on the flight. I still have my original paperback. I know all the stories, all the nicknames, everything that I'd ever need to know about the 1969 Seattle Pilots. After 32 readings or so of this sports classic, it's still a great way to open a baseball season, because "Ball Four" seems to be about baseball the way it ought to be. A lot of fun and laughs.

Well, maybe not exactly the way baseball ought to be, because in those days the players were practically the owners' indentured servants.

Of course, the 2003 baseball season might provide some fun, especially in New York. George Steinbrenner's Yankees are a favorite to get back into the Fall Classic. Fred Wilpon's Mets? Who knows? They have a lot of names. But the point is that New York baseball fans have something to root for, something to keep their interest.

In this way New York fans are lucky—whether they think so or not—because that's atypical of the average baseball fan across the country. The Oakland Athletics aficionado is at the other end of the spectrum. Baseball Commissioner Bud Selig undermined the legitimacy of the entire 2003 season last month when he suggested that a team like Oakland might still be a candidate for contraction, even though the agreement that the owners and players hammered out last August ensures that 30 teams will be competing through the length of the contract.

Striking a further blow, the Oakland ownership told its star player and American League MVP Miguel Tejada that it could not afford to pay him beyond this season. (Memo to Fred Wilpon: You can put Tejada in a Met uniform in 2004 after you dispose of Jeromy Burnitz's contract.)

The Tejada situation is exactly what is wrong with Major League Baseball. Oakland couldn't keep its best player, Jason Giambi, after the 2001 season and he ended up with the cash-rich George Steinbrenner Yankees. Oakland simply cannot compete with the Yankees or the Mets.

But Oakland isn't the only problem. Baseball can't find a suitable place to relocate the ownerless Montreal Expos. Portland, Ore., Washington, D.C., and northern Virginia want a shot at getting the Expos, but there is no money to build a baseball park in Portland, Washington wants to cap public investment in a baseball park, and it's been a slow go in Virginia to get funding for a stadium. (Another memo to Wilpon: Montreal's Vladimir Guerrero is a free agent after this season.)

In fact, baseball has become such a miserable investment that the man behind "Real Journalism" and "Fair and Balanced News" of the Fox News Channel, Rupert Murdoch, is selling his Los Angeles Dodgers. The Dodgers were once called "baseball's answer to the Denver mint."

Face it, the baseball business is bad all over. The Walt Disney Company reached baseball's pinnacle and won the 2002 World Series as owners of the Anaheim Angels. But Disney has been trying to sell the team for a while and still lacks a buyer.

AOL-Time Warner is in such bad shape that it may consider selling the Atlanta Braves. (Memo to Wilpon, buy this team—and close it.) The Cleveland Indians owner Larry Dolan has gutted the Indians because Cablevision's stock dropped so much that he can't make any real investments in players. Meanwhile, cash-starved teams in Kansas City, Pittsburgh, San Diego, Cincinnati, Florida, Montreal, Toronto and Milwaukee (home of Bud Selig's Brewers) cannot compete for a playoff spot on a regular basis—so much for their beleagured faithful.

Occasionally lightning strikes and a small market like Oakland or Minnesota fields a good team, but in the long run these franchises can't hold onto their big names. And that means Steinbrenner and Wilpon can gobble up top players because their TV monies give them such a high stream of revenue.

Given the sorry plight of the national pastime, Selig has come up with a task force to solve baseball's problems and he has gone to the bullpen to bring in his closer, George Will.

The conservative columnist is Selig's ace in the hole. He was one of four people on Selig's Blue Ribbon Committee studying the game's economics in 2000 and, in Selig's mind, Will brings a lot of gravitas to the game.

Will will be joined by the A-list of baseball insiders, including the heads of ESPN, FOX, academics from the Wharton Business School and Northwestern, and former players. But the task force does not include any paying customers; no Bleacher Creatures from Yankee Stadium or Mets fans who take the No. 7 train to Flushing.

Selig's task force is comprised of the people (the TV network heads, the players association, the Wills of the world) who no doubt put baseball in the bad economic position it finds itself in.

By the way, Jim Bouton is not on that task force, either. Typical baseball. "Ball Four" is on the New York Public Library's list of the most influential books written in the 20th Century. Bouton must know something about baseball. Certainly more than George Will.

The Pastime is Beginning to Look Past Its Prime
Newsday, New York City Edition, July 15, 2003

Can you picture this? New York Yankees owner George Steinbrenner giving a pep talk to the American League All-Stars, telling the players they must win tonight's annual exhibition game in Chicago because his Yankees need home-field advantage in the World Series.

If they tune him out, maybe he can pin his hopes for the post-season on the Mets closer Armando Benitez coming into the ninth inning to "save" it for the National League. Yeah, that's a better bet.

Wait a second...just why are Commissioner Bud Selig, Major League Baseball and the Major League Players Association letting the All-Star Game affect the franchise's most cherished crown jewel, the World Series?

That's an easy one. Baseball thinks more people will watch it on TV if something is riding on the outcome. The 2002 All-Star Game, which ended abruptly in an 11-inning tie after the Yankee skipper Joe Torre and Arizona Diamondbacks manager Bob Brenley told Selig they'd run out of pitchers, drew about 10 million viewers—a far cry from the 20 million people who watched the 1982 contest—the highest number in 21 years.

The major leagues are eager to reverse the slide in the country's consciousness. Baseball has wrapped itself around the flag to the point where "God Bless America" is played during the seventh-inning stretch at every game. But its rather bizarre moves in hopes of getting more young people interested in its product do make one wonder about Selig, his fellow owners and the industry's marketing people, and whether they really believe that the actual game of baseball, as it's played on the field, is still a drawing card.

It appears that the national pastime has been hijacked by two Australian TV executives. News Corp. CEO Rupert Murdoch and Fox Sports President David Hill wanted to boost Fox's TV ratings, so now there's a gimmick and a slogan, "This Time It Counts," to make sure that even couch potatoes get the message.

But awarding the home-field advantage to a league, not a team, on the basis of an exhibition game cheapens the post-season.

Baseball should be giving the team with the best record the home town crowd in the World Series, as it does in the first two play-off rounds. Since 1903, baseball has been alternating the home-field advantage. In 2001, the National League had the extra game, and Arizona won Game Seven over Steinbrenner's Yankees in the bottom of the ninth inning.

So should the Yankees or, by some miracle, the Mets, end up in a Game Seven at home, based on a July promotion event, rather than on the basis of having the best record over a 162-game schedule? This marketing ploy raises questions about the industry's integrity and credibility.

And so does another weird marketing development that Selig and his cohorts have come up with—becoming an associate sponsor of the Ozzfest 2003 concert tour. Major League Baseball Properties has signed a deal with Clear Channel Entertainment (the people who bring us Rush Limbaugh's radio show) in a dubious attempt to bring new fans to the game.

It's an unlikely pairing, no matter how you score it. Ozzy Osbourne is a heavy-metal performer who has a legendary history of substance abuse. He and his mates don't quite fit baseball's clean-cut image of itself. Do the major leagues really want to associate with Ozzy? They have enough trouble with corked bats and falling sausages.

The answer, however, is yes, because people know Osbourne and his family from their popular MTV show (just renewed for a fourth season) and it allows baseball to sell some merchandise at the Ozzfest concerts. The Ozzfest crowd is the group that Vince McMahon and World Wrestling Entertainment apparently lust after. Now Bud Selig is lusting after them, too.

Surprisingly, Ozzy and Major League Baseball do have a few things in common. Like baseball, Ozzy's star seems to be fading, as the Osbourne's MTV show has seen its ratings tumble. The eccentric Osbourne family doesn't seem so cute since Ozzy's 17-year-old son Jack has gone through substance-abuse rehab. Baseball's home-run records don't seem so hot either with the Cubs' Sammy Sosa being caught with an illegal bat, along with the never-ending stories of athletes' ephedra and steroid abuse.

What would baseball want with a heavy-metal festival featuring the likes of Marilyn Manson and Korn? Why would baseball want to cheapen its World Series by pinning home-field advantage on an exhibition game? It's because baseball's thinkers have lost sight of the fact that the game is the thing. Baseball markets everything but baseball.

And that's the kind of thinking that should convince George Steinbrenner to address the American League squad before tonight's game in Chicago. Game Seven is on the line for the Yankees.

Pete Rose May Have Gambled on Baseball...
NBCSports.com, January 4, 2004

Major League Baseball is all set to make the Hall of Fame announcement on Tuesday afternoon on its website. Who will be the new honorees? That's a secret, but everyone in the baseball world knows who won't be selected.

Pete Rose is still in baseball's version of Elba, waiting in exile for a call from Baseball Commissioner Bud Selig saying that all is forgiven. And maybe all will be forgiven after Rose's book comes out if he thoroughly and truthfully explains his betting habits.

Rose was removed "for acts that stained the game" back on August 24, 1989. Just what those acts were is an official Major League Baseball secret, although it's commonly thought that Rose bet on baseball, which is, of course, taboo.

Rose was permanently banned from the baseball industry, not just Major League Baseball. But why he was given the boot remains something of a mystery. Officially, then commissioner A. Bartlett Giamatti tossed Rose with a rather ambiguous statement concerning an agreement between Rose's advisors and baseball.

"Nothing in this agreement shall be deemed either an admission or a denial by Peter Edward Rose of the allegation that he bet on any major league baseball game." But Giamatti told reporters he had concluded that Rose placed bets on baseball games. Giamatti died eight days after the Rose ruling. The next commissioner, Fay Vincent, a close friend of Giamatti, refused to pardon Rose.

Now it's Bud Selig's decision. But is Bud Selig the right man to make the call on Rose, and has Selig done more harm to baseball than Rose? Selig's record as the Milwaukee Brewers owner should be scrutinized. In 1988, the Players Association charged that the 26 owners got together and acted in collusion to depress salaries, a violation of the collective bargaining agreement.

The case went before arbitrator Thomas Roberts, who agreed with the players. Eventually, the owners settled the grievance by agreeing to pay $280 million in damages to the players. Selig was one of the 26 owners who, to use a Giamatti quote, stained the game.

In 1994, the players walked off the job. Selig, then the acting commissioner, cancelled the World Series and promised replacement baseball using minor leaguers and semi-pro players for the 1995 season. The players ended their strike on March 31, 1995 when judge Sonia Sotomayer of the U.S. District Court in Manhattan ruled that the owners bargained in bad faith.

Roughly at the same time that Sotomayer came down with her ruling, Selig began to campaign for a new stadium for his Milwaukee Brewers. Selig lost his first go round when Wisconsin voters said no to a new ballpark, but he continued to lobby Madison legislators and eventually a new stadium bill was passed, with the bulk of the money for the facility coming from a sales tax hike in the five counties surrounding Milwaukee. Selig had pledged that the Brewers would be competitive with a new stadium and needed a new stadium to keep up with other teams.

Wisconsin legislators and residents were stunned this fall to read that the Brewers, who are being run by Selig's daughter, were cutting payroll and trading away the team's top moneymakers because the franchise was having financial woes. This only three years after the Brewers opened the new park.

Selig was also the point man in the 2001 "contraction" talks when MLB threatened to put two teams out of business. One of the teams on the chopping block was Minnesota, and a Minnesota judged ordered the Twins to honor their lease in 2002. Selig was still on the contraction bandwagon in February 2003 even though the collective bargaining agreement called for 30 Major League teams during the life of the deal. Selig in a speech told Oakland businessmen that the A's were a contraction candidate.

Rose may have bet on baseball but he ended up doing a lot more harm to himself than the game. Selig and his owners have done much more to "stain the game."

It's time to let Pete into the Hall of Fame and for someone other than Selig and his baseball advisors to make the decision on Pete Rose's future baseball role.

Bring the A's Back to Philly
Metro [Philly], April 29, 2004

Just in case you haven't noticed, the Major League Baseball team formerly known as the Philadelphia Athletics is still looking for a permanent home since leaving Shibe Park/Connie Mack Stadium at the end of the 1954 season.

That brief sojourn in Kansas City from 1955 to 1967 didn't work out nor did the 1968 move to Oakland. The current A's ownership in Oakland would like to pick up the franchise and move it to say San Jose or Santa Clara but the San Francisco Giants brass along with Baseball Commissioner Bud Selig won't give their blessings to the idea even though Oakland is significantly closer to San Francisco than Santa Clara or San Jose.

The two South Bay Area communities are part of the San Francisco Giants franchise territory even though voters in both areas turned down then Giants owner Bob Lurie's request for a new stadium in stadium referendum proposals in the 1980s. It would be interesting and intriguing if the A's ownership decided to sue baseball in an effort move to San Jose or Santa Clara and see what sort of strategy Selig, Bob Dupuy and Major League Baseball would use in trying to stop the team formerly known as the Philadelphia A's from moving.

But here's an idea for A's owners Steve Schott and Kenneth Hoffman. Move the team back to Philadelphia. Bring the A's back. After all the Phillies will honor the old American League franchise in the team's new, taxpayers' funded stadium. The A's and Phillies used to share Shibe Park and Philadelphia could use the extra revenue that a second baseball team could generate to pay off all of those bills at the new and very expensive stadium.

Philadelphia is Major League Baseball's largest one team market and, back in 2000, a blue ribbon committee looking into the future suggested that MLB move financially struggling teams into big markets to both increase the struggling team's bottom line and also siphon off revenue from large market teams. Philadelphia was once an American League town. It was Connie Mack who sublet Shibe Park to the Phillies; it was the A's who won World Series, not the Phillies.

Of course, bringing the A's back to Philadelphia would have to start with someone convincing Mayor Street and Gov. Rendell that putting a second team in Philadelphia would be a good idea. Then it would require the Phillies to give up their baseball exclusivity in the new stadium and sharing revenues derived from luxury boxes, club seats, concessions and parking. Then there is a matter of cable TV. Would Comcast want a second baseball team in the market? Would the cable giant, which is partners with the Phillies, want competition? Would a Philadelphia A's team get a deal with Comcast or have to start a new cable network and beg Comcast for channel space? Would corporate Philadelphia buy into a second team?

After all of that is done, there is still one remaining question. Will a second team attract rank and file, common fans? After all, corporate businesses buy up luxury boxes and club seats as a business lure or a tax write off, but would baseball fans accept the return of the Philadelphia A's?

The answer would be yes, but it's a question that will never be answered because of an anti-trust exemption. The baseball monopoly won't allow Philadelphia to become a two-market city again.

Even if NHL Owners Lock Out Players, New League Not Viable

NBCSports.com, August 30, 2004

The Quebec Nordiks are history, teen-age phonon Sidney Crosby has said thanks but no thanks to the Hamilton franchise's three-year, $7.5 million offer and WHA officials vehemently denied media reports that they are in negotiations with the NHL regarding a potential sale of the World Hockey Association to the NHL. Of course there isn't very much to the WHA except the trademark World Hockey Association name that the NHL didn't bother to buy when it "expanded" to four WHA cities—Edmonton, Winnipeg, Quebec City and Hartford—in 1979.

As the calendar flips to September, the WHA appears to be far more of a dream than a reality. The league should be getting ready for training camps and its first game, but there is no evidence that the league has even signed contracts with any rinks for practice time. And the league's first face off has been pushed back from an October start to sometime in November.

The WHA had some grand plans. The founders apparently did not bother to study wreckages of the XFL and the Women's United Soccer Association (WUSA). Both the XFL and the WUSA had major television backing. The XFL had NBC and Viacom behind it; the WUSA had a consortium of cable television companies behind it.

Both failed.

The WHA apparently is soldiering on, but the grandiose plans of a 12-team North American league as well as a European division and a junior league are apparently just that—grandiose plans. At this point, with the NHL owners and players associations heading toward a lockout, the WHA's timing to fill the void left by labor strife is the only thing working in its favor.

The league has not sold a ticket, has no network or cable TV deals, no players, no referees, and apparently it has just one team employee. The Detroit Gladiators, who are scheduled to be playing in the Detroit Lions' old Silverdome home field in Pontiac, Mich., have a coach, former NHL defenseman Moe Mantha.

The league could have teams in Halifax, Nova Scotia; Vancouver, British Columbia; and Dallas. The Toronto franchise has no place to play nor does the Hamilton team. It's unclear whether or not the Halifax franchise has a lease agreement to use the city's arena. The Gladiators have a Web site, the Dallas Americans have a lease agreement with the city to use Reunion Arena.

Dallas does have a team though, the Americans, and Vancouver will be known by its old WHA name, the Blazers. The NHL didn't bother taking that name either in 1979.

The Quebec City is just the latest franchise that has folded. In June, a Calgary, Alberta, company purchased two franchises, one in Jacksonville, Fla., and the other in Orlando, Fla., from David Waronker. Waronker's teams had been in the WHA2, a low-level minor league that is now the Southern Professional Hockey League. Waronker claimed he never got the money for the teams and called off the deal. A few weeks later, Waronker was again thinking of placing his Orlando team in the WHA, but that fell through.

The WHA held its first, and more than likely its last, amateur and professional drafts in mid-July at a casino in Niagara Falls, Ontario. The league's so-called commissioner, Bobby Hull, stormed out after getting questions from reporters about the league's viability. Hull really isn't the commissioner and seems to be available to the league in some sort of public relations deal a few times a month.

The WHA's initial goal was to be a notch under the NHL, but better than the top hockey minor league, the American Hockey League. The founders wanted to put excitement back in hockey with rules designed to promote more scoring. Prices would bring more families into arenas, although the average ticket was going to be more than $30 per game.

The WHA made a number of mistakes. Hockey is growing quickly in the United States. USA Hockey has more members than ever before, the NHL has 24 U.S. teams, and the minor leagues continue to grow, particularly in the south. The United States has a successful national team now that is being fed by junior leagues that are sprouting up throughout the country.

There is really no need for an alternate "major league" in the United States. The WHA founders learned that the other cities that had a remote interest in the WHA were those with old and unused arenas like Dallas and Pontiac. The WHA was reduced to looking for those type of venues, but could not land Miami or Cincinnati or at basketball facilities in Phoenix or Minneapolis.

In Canada, the league may have landed Halifax, which is too small, and not economically robust enough to compete with say, Toronto, and failed in Quebec City. Toronto and Hamilton have various levels of hockey ranging from the NHL to the AHL to juniors. There really is no need for the WHA, even if NHL owners lock out their players, the American Hockey League will be playing, as will the ECHL, the United Hockey League, the Western Professional Hockey League and the Southern Professional Hockey League. Additionally, there is college hockey, and junior development leagues such as the United States Hockey League and the North American Hockey League. And a few U.S. cities have Canadian Junior A Hockey teams. There is plenty of hockey available in the lower 48 and Alaska even if the NHL does lock out its players.

In 1971, there was a need for the original WHA which opened southern markets, hired European players on a regular basis and gave hockey people jobs. The original WHA wasn't the best hockey nor were its teams well financed, but it pushed the NHL into changing its business strategies just like the American Football League did to the NFL and the American Basketball Association did to the NBA. But in 1971, when the original WHA organizers started thinking about starting play in 1972, the NHL had 14 teams. Today it has 30, USA Hockey is an international force, there are minor leagues, development leagues and hockey programs from the ages of 5 to juniors. There just isn't any need for the WHA as its organizers are finding out.

Baseball is Back, Anyone Recognize it?

Washington Examiner, April 13, 2005

For those who happened to see the Washington Senators' last game back on Sept. 30, 1971, and plan on seeing a Nationals game sometime this year, the only resemblance between Major League Baseball in 1971 and in 2005 is the name Major League Baseball.

The entire business has done a 180-degree turn.

When Bob Short decided to relocate his Senators to Arlington, Texas, in September of 1971, there were just 24 teams.

Curt Flood, who had sued Major League Baseball over its labor practices and the Reserve Clause after being traded by St. Louis to Philadelphia following the 1969 season, played 13 games for the Senators before retiring. If a player was traded, he could not refuse the trade and had to stay with a club for the entire length of his career unless the club decided it was time to get rid of him.

Cable TV was in its infancy with just a few systems across the country dabbling in sports. Baseball depended on national TV monies from NBC, local TV and radio monies, and the average blue-collar worker to buy tickets, with the high rollers buying box seats near the field. The difference in cost between the box seat and the second tier seat was minimal, maybe a dollar or two.

When Short left in 1971, the game was in the midst of sweeping changes. But baseball owners probably didn't realize how the entire industry was going to be affected within a matter of five years. Short moved the team based on poor attendance.

Attendance made or broke a team.

Poor attendance was the reason behind Calvin Griffith's move of the Senators to Minnesota after the 1960 season.

Had Short stayed in Washington, the Senators might have had better days. But Short didn't wait for the Metro to open. Short did not foresee that the explosion in national, local and cable TV revenues was just around the corner. That marketing and sponsorship deals would bring in millions upon millions of dollars. That cities would put up hundreds of millions of dollars to build ballparks and allow team owners to keep the lion's share of the revenues generated within the facility.

Baseball sells the logo and builds up brand names like the Washington Nationals. Players come and go. A team's name, uniform and logo, which are carefully researched and put before focus groups, are now the selling points.

It's an entirely different game in 2005. Ballparks have restaurants, bars, business centers for business people. Fans are segregated with the high rollers getting separate entrances to the equivalent of gated communities, whether it is luxury boxes or club seats near the field. In some ways, the game is an afterthought and may be the least important part of the entire baseball experience.

And for those who have not seen a Major League Baseball game since Sept. 30, 1971, the only constants in the past 33 years are that the mound is 60 feet, six inches from the plate and the bases are 90 feet apart.

Everything else has changed.

Colleges

Big Money Throws College Sports for a Loss
Newsday, October 14, 2003

There won't be Midnight Madness this year on the St. John's campus in Queens. No raucous student pep rallies for the Red Storm when the clock strikes 12:01 a.m. on Oct. 17, the time that the National Collegiate Athletic Association has designated as the official start of the college basketball season.

Somehow, it is fitting that St. John's isn't holding its traditional Midnight Madness session. After all, St. John's doesn't really know what its basketball future will look like next year—and that has nothing to do with its coaching staff or its players.

In the world of college sports in 2003, the least important part of the product is the actual athletic competition. St. John's was a founding member of the Big East Conference, a basketball league that became a big-time football conference because of TV and money. St. John's basketball is in trouble because the college sports industry is driven by football and the university doesn't have a big-time football program.

If St. John's wasn't located in New York, the school would be just another university with a small-time program. Because the Red Storm plays in Madison Square Garden, St. John's remains a player on the national level. Once school is done next May, three Big East football teams, Boston College, Miami and Virginia Tech, are leaving to join the Atlantic Coast Conference for the promise of millions of dollars in TV money. The departures could devastate the Big East, and the conference could lose its spot in college football's Bowl Championship Series, where the really big money is made.

The Big East is suing the nine-team Atlantic Coast Conference, accusing it of conspiring to ruin the Big East. But it's unclear if Miami and Virginia Tech did anything wrong when they accepted ACC invitations, followed by Boston College. Meanwhile, the Big East is apparently ready to raid other conferences to replace its losses and maintain its position.

Big-time college sports are all about money, and that has drawn the attention of the House Judiciary Committee. But the House committee missed a golden opportunity to get to the bottom of the college sports industry's problems when it held a hearing on college sports last month.

Rep. John Conyers (D-Mich.) asked the committee to investigate the College Football Bowl Championship Series arrangement and the circumstances behind the Atlantic Coast Conference's "expansion."

Conyers wanted to know why, since the founding of the Bowl Championship Series in 1998, the vast majority of the proceeds and power has been concentrated among 63 schools in six major conferences (the Atlantic Coast Conference, Pacific-10, Big Ten, Southeastern, Big 12 and Big East). In 2002–03 only $5 million out of a total revenue of $109 million went to non-bowl championship series colleges.

Conyers should have called the heads of big-time college sports schools and asked why they are handing out multi-million-dollar contracts to football and basketball coaches while tuition is soaring for non-athletes. Conyers should have inquired about the practice of not insuring athletes against injuries suffered in "voluntary" off-season practices, of students' being unable to work under NCAA rules if they have an athletic scholarship and the fact that most athletes are too busy playing sports to get a good education.

It's time to stop pretending that Division I college football and basketball are some sort of amateur or scholastic endeavor for students. It's a big-time professional operation that allows schools, coaches and TV networks to earn big dollars.

Colleges and universities are supposed to be places where students matriculate and get ready for the real world. For Division I schools, though, the real world is filling stadiums and arenas with well-heeled boosters, signing deals with corporations for stadium-naming rights, getting money from shoe companies for outfitting their teams, and putting the best product available on the field to justify the multi-million-dollar broadcasting contracts for their games.

Of course, college athletes get little more than a scholarship to attend the school. And attend is the operative word here because there are many schools that aren't graduating their football and basketball players. Even if so-called student athletes want to go to class, they are somewhat restricted because of long daily practices and travel.

It's only a matter of time before those 63 Bowl Championship Series football schools break off to form their own semi-pro league, leaving schools like St. John's behind. Maybe then Conyers and his colleagues will finally ask the right questions about the "madness" of the college sports industry.

Football Fanatics Flock Here to Catch a Draft
Newsday, New York City Edition, April 22, 2003

If you happen to be walking near Madison Square Garden on Saturday morning, you might see hordes of characters, some dressed in black looking a lot like Darth Vader and others looking like space aliens with green or blue faces, wandering around somewhat lost.

No, it's not a sign that Halloween has come early, but it is a signal that Americans are ready to turn away from the war in Iraq and revel in the future battles of the gridiron. Yes, it's that time of year when football fans come out of hibernation in their best tailgate-stadium attire to celebrate what is essentially a restraint of trade, the NFL draft.

It doesn't matter to NFL fanatics that the baseball season is nearly a month old or that the NBA and NHL are in their playoffs. No, it's time to salute the most perfect form of socialism ever invented. The National Football League, where all 32 owners share money, has devised a way of divvying up college athletes that under most other circumstances would be illegal.

And the fans buy into the notion and don't ask questions. Everybody gets their football fix—from Jets and Giants fans, to the Buffalo Bills Backers and the Cleveland Browns Backers, as well as Green Bay Packers "cheeseheads" and die-hard members of the Raider Nation, to name but a few. They get to attend a football function that's a lot like the old Jerry Seinfeld show where nothing happens, at least not at the Garden.

The football fanatics can't tailgate because you can't do that sort of thing along 33rd Street or 31st Street or 7th and 8th Avenue, especially now. So they go inside wearing their nutty outfits, read what Mel Kiper Jr., or anyone of literally 200 other draft gurus have to say about the NFL's potential new employees, and jump up and down hoping that an ESPN camera will put their mugs on cable TV. It's like the crowd on "Let's Make a Deal."

They sit around and wait for the NFL Commissioner Paul Tagliabue to announce that the Cincinnati Bengals are "on the clock." Each team has 15 minutes to makes its picks in the first round. The commissioner will make his little speech and the fans will scream and then sit on their hands until Tagliabue calls the first name selected. The top prospective employees sit within ESPN's camera range and when an athlete's name is announced, ESPN captures the Kodak moment and the fanatics react the way Caesar might have. With a thumbs up or a thumbs down.

Of course, all this hoopla ultimately signifies nothing. Jet fans scream "J-E-T-S, JETS, JETS, JETS!" They hope the team drafts the right player but they are generally going to be disappointed because the brass goes after the player they think is the best, not the fan favorites. Giants fans can be equally vocal. Once, they booed the team when it drafted Phil Simms, a little-known quarterback from Moorehead State in Kentucky, in the first round in 1979. They all remember the name now—he won the Giants a Superbowl.

It's a tough crowd. But the fans really don't know how tough it is inside their favorite team's "war room." Spread across the country in each city that has a franchise, the war room resembles the old smoke-filled backroom at a political convention. Each team has a place filled with coaches and scouts arguing among themselves, and on the rare occasion, even getting physical, while discussing the merits of a particular player. Teams will attempt to trade players for better placement in the draft and will make a deal just to snatch a player if they get wind that another team is honing in on their top choice.

Some organizations have accused others of bugging their war rooms to find out what is going on. The NFL draft really is crisis time. After all, teams are investing millions of dollars in first-round picks and a "bust" could force an upset owner to fire his entire personnel department, from the general manager to the coach to even the public relations man.

At this coming draft, the Jets' Terry Bradway should be looking for defenders, as will the Giants' Ernie Accorsi. Once the top five or six players are taken, the boredom should kick in for the Garden spectators. But it doesn't. The fanatics stay glued to the in-house ESPN feed where analysts at various NFL team war rooms report and basically have nothing to say. Come to think of it, those analysts seem to resemble the retired generals discussing war strategy.

In essence, the NFL owners have perfected a system to the point where they don't have to compete for the very top college students who are eager to enter their unique business world, professional football. The teams automatically get the top applicants. Imagine accounting companies just going to Wharton or Harvard School of Business and drafting students. It can't be done.

Yet the NFL draft is legal because the owners' and the players' associations have cut a deal that allows the draft to be legal, even though college players apparently are left with few rights.

The college players buy into the notion that they don't need choices. And maybe the top players don't because they are guaranteed millions of dollars in signing bonuses after they are drafted. Those students leaving school are in much better shape than their non-football player peers who are struggling to find jobs and internships during President George W. Bush's stewardship of the faltering economy. They should all be so lucky. The 250 or so drafted players are guaranteed jobs. Whether they keep their positions depends on how well they do once they report next month.

Football players' contracts are not guaranteed, but they do keep the bonuses. Chosen college applicants are also slotted into a sliding salary scale. The No. 1 pick will get the most money, the final player chosen gets the least. But at least the last player picked in the draft gets a week vacation in Newport Beach, Calif., as the Lowsman Trophy winner.

The geo-political world has changed since March 19, but not the football world. Some things just never change.

Treat NCAA Like Big Business
Metro [Philly], June 17, 2003

You would hope Sen. Arlen Spector has more important issues to tackle than what college is in what sports conference. But Senator Spector along with eight of his colleagues sent a letter to University of Miami President Donna Shalala, the former Secretary of Health and Human Services in the Clinton Administration, as well as to the Syracuse University Chancellor and the Boston College President begging them to keep their schools in the Big East Conference.

Why should Arlen Spector and his fellow Senators care about college football games? Because it's all about money and misplaced priorities.

In a show of bi-partisan strength, Senators Joseph Lieberman and Christopher Dodd of Connecticut; Jon Corzine and Frank Lautenberg of New Jersey; Jay Rockefeller and Robert Byrd of West Virginia; John Warner and George Allen of Virginia; and Spector wrote if those three schools bolt the Big East for a promise of more money to join the Atlantic Coast Conference it would "send a troubling message to student-athletes across America."

Here's some news for the senators. Big time college sports are about money and football.

It's time to stop pretending that Division 1 college football and basketball are some sort of amateur or scholastic endeavor for students. It's a big-time professional operation where everyone from schools to coaches to TV networks make big dollars. Everyone that is except for the performers, the teenagers and young adults who play the games that attract people to the arenas and stadiums or to watch them on television.

Colleges are supposed to be places where students matriculate and get ready for the real world where football should be a social activity. But, for Division 1 schools, though, the real world is filling stadiums and arenas with well-heeled boosters, signing deals with corporations for stadium naming rights, getting money from shoe companies for outfitting their teams, and putting the best product available on the field so that ESPN, ABC, NBC, CBS, FOX and

FOX Sports Net can dole out multi-million dollar contracts for their games.

While all of this is going on, Division 1 college athletes are getting nothing but a scholarship to attend the school. And "attend" is the operative word here because there are many schools that aren't graduating their football and basketball players.

Athletes are prohibited from holding down jobs while they play. Even if so-called student athletes want to go to class, they are somewhat restricted because of long, daily practices and travel.

The athletes are responsible for billion dollar TV deals for the NCAA Basketball Tournaments, multi-million dollar national and local cable and broadcast TV deals, yet they don't see a penny from any of the contracts that college and university presidents along with athletic directors approve.

Spector and his colleagues should rein in big-time college sports, take tax breaks away and demand that the stars of the show, the athletes, get their fair share. Big time college sports have run amok. It's time to come clean and admit that Division 1 football and basketball are nothing more than minor league proving grounds for players and moneymaking ventures for everyone else.

California Bill Has NCAA Quaking

Metro [Philly], November 18, 2003

Temple Owls Basketball Coach John Chaney, Saint Joseph's University counterpart Phil Martelli along with the coaches from Drexel, La Salle, Penn, Temple, and Villanova should consider scheduling a round robin tournament in Sacramento, Calif. and stop by the office of Gov. Arnold Schwarzenegger. The six coaches may have to turn lobbyists and stop The Terminator from possibly terminating the NCAA as it exists today.

The California Senate has approved a bill co-sponsored by Culver City Democrat Kevin Murray and San Francisco Democrat John Burton that has put the NCAA on notice. The two state Senators want the NCAA to start paying California athletes, who play for 47 colleges and universities, for their time on the football field, basketball court or baseball diamond. The bill will be considered by the California Assembly, and if passed will go to Governor Schwarzenegger's desk for his consideration.

Murray's concern is not with the schools, but with the players. He wants them to get some compensation for their work and have the right to have representation. The schools trade a scholarship for sports participation.

What that means is an athlete can participate in sports but generally cannot work and earn money while he or she is performing during the season. There are some other grants available as well, but for the most part so-called student-athletes have work restrictions placed on them that no other college student has. The football and basketball players receive little compensation in comparison to coaches who are getting millions of dollars from the schools, television partners and from endorsements.

Basketball players have to wear a sneaker from the shoe company that has hired their coach as an endorser.

The NCAA, the presidents and athletic directors of big time sports playing schools, the cable and broadcasting networks, advertisers, marketing partners, and boosters want no part of the Murray-Burton bill because it would break up their gravy train.

Remember schools, broadcast and cable partners, advertisers, sneaker companies and coaches are making a lot of money off the backs of the football and basketball players at the schools. The reconfiguration of athletic conferences came after the Atlantic Coast Conference decided to "invite" the University of Miami, Boston College and Syracuse into their conference to bolster their TV markets, giving the conference the New York, Boston and Miami markets which would help them get more money from CBS, NBC, ABC (ESPN) or FOX.

What happens if some of that money is diverted into player salaries? What happens if California, with high profile schools like Stanford, USC and UCLA, requires players to be paid and the NCAA drops those 47 schools from it membership? What happens when other states follow California's lead and introduce similar legislation? It would fracture the NCAA's sponsor and marketing relationships because the California market would be gone. That's one-fifth of the country and includes two of the nation's top five TV markets in Los Angeles and the San Francisco Bay Area.

The California Assembly and "The Terminator" could alter the big-time college sports industry and that California earthquake would cause tremors and shockwaves in places as far away as Harrisburg and Philadelphia.

Ethical Problems Plague Sports

Metro [Philly Weekend], December 31, 2003–January 4, 2004

College football's Bowl Championship Series has survived two Congressional hearings about its set up this year but sports announcers, sportswriters and fans are now criticizing the BCS because computers may have come up with the wrong conclusion. The BCS's computer has placed Louisiana State University and Oklahoma in the designated championship game, the Sugar Bowl, in New Orleans instead of slotting the University of Southern California in that contest. Southern California is thought by many to be college football's best team but the school isn't playing in the championship game.

Southern California will compete in the Rose Bowl in Pasadena, Calif., instead, but college football and big time college sports in general have far more problems than having a computer coming up with the wrong match up in a championship game.

Big time college sports has had a horrible 2003. Numerous scandals surrounded quite a few basketball teams, ranging from the suspensions of 12 Villanova basketball players for unauthorized use of a telephone access code to call off-campus locations, to the use of academically ineligible players at St. Bonaventure, to the murder of a Baylor University player and Baylor University's coach Dave Bliss trying to invent a story to cover his tracks in an investigation of the entire program. The University of Cincinnati basketball coach Bob Huggins still has not graduated a player from the program.

Misdeeds have not been limited to just basketball programs. Big time college and university presidents, chancellors and other people in very important positions have orchestrated conference switches designed to maximize rights fees from cable and over-the-air television networks. The Atlantic Coast Conference, which consisted of nine teams in the southeast, decided to raid three "big" market Big East Conference teams, Boston College, Syracuse University and Miami, so the conference would be in a better position with "new" markets in Boston, New York and South Florida and also to create a conference football championship game. The two moves went hand in hand and were set up to bring in more money to ACC programs.

The Big East, aided by Connecticut and Pennsylvania's Attorney Generals, went to court and sued the ACC, claiming that the ACC, Miami, and Boston College conspired to destroy its conference. The ACC then "invited" Virginia Tech and Miami to join the conference and forgot about Syracuse and Boston College. Eventually Boston College jumped conferences and the lawsuit continues.

Pennsylvania Attorney General Mike Fisher joined in the lawsuit to "protect" Pennsylvania taxpayers who invested money in the University of Pittsburgh's athletic programs by helping to fund a new football stadium for the Panthers and the Pittsburgh Steelers and a new basketball arena on the campus. Fisher argued that the school could lose millions of dollars if the ACC were allowed to "dismember" the Big East.

Meanwhile, the Big East "raided" Conference USA taking four schools and that set off a domino affect with other conferences "inviting" schools to come along. Also, the Auburn University president was forced to make a public apology for having a secret meeting with Louisville football coach Bobby Petrino in an attempt to hire him while Tommy Tuberville had a job. Auburn recently extended Tuberville's contract.

People and Pennsylvania taxpayers shouldn't be too concerned that a computer slipped up and didn't put the best team in the championship football game. It is really a minor bump in the road compared to college sports industry's ethical problems.

Get Serious About Cleaning Up College Athletics
Orlando Sentinel, May 20, 2004

It's May. It's graduation time for college students and maybe even some big-time college athletes who played college football or basketball in Florida schools. Maybe. The National Collegiate Athletic Association claims it is going to get tough on its members and wants, in the words of NCAA President Myles Brand, "to hold institutions and teams accountable for the academic progress of their student-athletes."

That is a laudable goal. Quite a concept as a matter of fact. Have schools whose charge is to educate students, educate students who happen to be majoring in football or basketball.

Of course, the NCAA has no idea exactly what it will do to a school like the University of Cincinnati that has not graduated a basketball player in years. Eventually, schools will pay the price for not educating players, but that is a problem to be solved down the road, not in 2004. Still, the NCAA would like to see more student-athletes get sheepskins like others who pay good money to matriculate at those institutions.

There are some obstacles that need to be overcome. Big-time college presidents and chancellors might have to say no to talented people who don't belong in a classroom, then they might have to mollify, in no particular order, boosters, donors, politicians, sneaker companies, other advertising partners, cable TV and over-the-air TV networks and TV stations, radio networks and local radio stations, luxury-box holders and lifetime seat holders. Those people who invest in a college program are more interested in the final score than the graduation percentage. The newly reconstituted Atlantic Coast Conference isn't getting millions upon millions of TV dollars to field subpar teams and TV executives who run both pro and college sports are not going to accept poor ratings, so immediately there is pressure on ACC member schools to be good in football and basketball.

Here are some suggestions for reform. Schools should admit that many of the players in big-time college sports are pros in training and that big-time college sports is a big business. Some of the players brought into a program are nothing more than hired hands whose job is to promote the school through their play.

The NCAA and college programs wield an iron fist when it comes to players' rights. Yes, scholarship players do have an opportunity to get an education, and some do take advantage of the offer. But they are players first and have to devote hours to their sport during the season and then have to prepare for their sport during the off-season. The NCAA needs to allow students to be students and get away from their sport to study and do away with so-called voluntary off-season practices. And if they don't, at least the schools should provide insurance for those taking part in off-season activities. Schools should honor commitments and not use a permanent injury as a reason for taking away a scholarship from a player who is physically unable to play because of an injury suffered while performing for the school.

The college presidents look rather hypocritical when they realign sports conferences to maximize TV dollars for their schools, yet they won't allow student-athletes to take jobs to support themselves. There needs to be an elimination of the $2,000 annual salary cap on money earned from legitimate employment. This has led some lawmakers, who don't trust the NCAA's intentions, to think about imposing regulations on the NCAA to protect students' rights. In California and Nebraska, the state legislatures are considering bills that would force schools to pay their players.

College athletes are exploited under the present system. There should be many more student-athletes marching with their peers in May graduations. The NCAA is claiming that big-time sports-playing schools really want to graduate players. If that is true, the NCAA should clean up its industry; if not, the schools should stop the student-athlete pretense and just admit what most people know. College football and basketball players are pros in training. They are nothing more than unpaid and uneducated fund-raisers for their schools.

Guaranteed Shoe Money Working Against Stern, NBA

Metro [Philly], May 24, 2004

Adidas is making life for National Basketball Association Commissioner David Stern more difficult. Stern, you might remember, is trying to get a 20-year-old age minimum for entry into his league for a variety of reasons ranging from something about basketball players getting college educations to teenagers just aren't ready to play in the NBA.

Adidas, a sneaker company, thinks otherwise and has signed two high school players—Brooklyn's Sebastian Telfair and Josh Smith—to multi-year marketing deals. Both Telfair and Smith figure to be first round picks in the 2004 NBA Draft.

Telfair and Smith presumably will be multi-millionaires before they get their high school diplomas. But David Stern wants to stop future Lebron James, Telfairs and Smiths from entering his world and wants the National Basketball Players Association to roll over and give its approval to a restraint of trade just like the National Football League Players Association.

Whatever Stern's public reasons are, they don't add up. Eighteen and nineteen year olds are fighting wars in both Afghanistan and Iraq. Eighteen-year-old musicians can tour the country and be on stage or in movies. They can vote in elections. Why shouldn't they be allowed to play professional basketball?

It's all about money. The NBA guarantees its first round draft picks four-year deals. Thirty entry players know they will be getting millions of dollars and that makes it easy for a player to skip his "pro in training" college career and go into the NBA. Dallas Mavericks owner Mark Cuban, who more than likely will never be part of Stern's inner circle, thinks Stern is wasting his time trying to impose an age minimum; instead Cuban would like to get rid of the first round guaranteed contract. In Cuban's mind, the guaranteed dollars flashed in a teenagers eyes is a lot better deal than playing for a college that can only offer a scholarship.

From an NBA owner's standpoint, raising the age minimum makes an awful lot of sense. It's easier to judge a player if he becomes a free agent at say 23 or 24 than 21 or 22.

Stern isn't worried about only 18-year-old basketball players. Stern said last January that he also has some serious concerns about younger players after talking to the parents of 11 year-olds who say their children can dribble a basketball and plan to skip college to play in the NBA.

Apparently Stern is suffering from a case of guilt and doesn't want to be blamed if teenagers decide to devote their lives to the pursuit of basketball careers instead of concentrating on their studies.

Had Stern been the Education Secretary instead of the NBA Commissioner, his argument might be more compelling. But the reason why Stern wants teenagers out is simple.

It comes down to money.

Cash Grab Proves ACC Did It for the Money
Metro [Philly], June 14, 2004

If you don't think the Atlantic Coast Conference recent "expansion" was all about money, and nothing but money, think again.

This grouping of schools in the Southeast that included Clemson, Duke, Florida State, Georgia Tech, Maryland, North Carolina, NC State, Virginia and Wake Forest has added Boston College, the University of Miami and Virginia Tech; signed a big money seven-year deal with the Walt Disney Company to air games on ABC and cablecast other games on the various ESPN networks; and now has asked cities up and down the East Coast to make a bid to host the ACC football title game in 2005 and 2006.

The ACC football expansion was all about money. Football brings in the lion's share of TV money. An ACC bowl championship will bring at least $6 million into the 12 colleges.

The ACC doesn't have a team in the New York area, so East Rutherford (one of the bidding sites) would be a strange option but the now 12-team conference wants to have a New York presence because that's where the money is from cable, TV networks and Madison Avenue.

What the ACC has openly become is a professional sports league where the players might get an education in return for playing football or basketball.

The players are pros in training but the ACC schools will insist that their players are really student athletes. And the people who really need to be questioned about how the ACC became a professional league are the school presidents, chancellors and regents. The pursuit of money and recognition is far more important as a sales tool for those schools than education.

Schools should admit that many of the players in big-time college sports are pros in training and that big-time college sports is a big business with ties to network TV, radio, advertisers, boosters, marketing partners and corporations buying luxury boxes and club seats. Some of the players brought into a program are nothing more than hired hands whose job is to promote the school through their play.

The college presidents look rather hypocritical when they realign sports conferences to maximize TV dollars for their schools, yet they won't allow their student-athletes to take jobs to support themselves. There needs to be an elimination of the $2,000 annual salary cap on money earned from legitimate employment. This has led some lawmakers to think about imposing regulations on the NCAA to protect students' rights. In California and Nebraska, the state legislatures are considering bills that would force schools to pay their players.

College football is a big business, which is why the ACC without any teams in the New York-area has asked New Jersey to bid on its championship game.

A Reality Check As NBA Commissioner Says No to 18-Year-Olds
The Orlando Sentinel, June 29, 2005

It must be good to be National Basketball Association Commissioner David Stern. The NBA strongman snaps his fingers and the National Basketball Players Association Executive Director Billy Hunter jumps and agrees to a new collective bargaining agreement that says high-school graduates can no longer apply for a job in Stern's domain starting in 2006.

Stern doesn't want new high-school grads in his league because he says it's not good for his business.

But Stern will welcome 18-year-olds in his league for a final time in 2005–06. If any of them are any good, he will market their likenesses globally if the NBA can make a buck off them. Stern defends his hypocritical stance by saying that once a player joins the NBA, he has full membership rights.

Just as Stern got his way, the Pentagon decided to go after the same high-school-student pool that Stern decided was too young, immature and unproven for his franchise owners and the high rollers who buy NBA tickets whether they are in the comfort and safety of a luxury box or sitting in seats with WiFi-equipped waiter service.

Stern repeatedly said that there is no room for recent high-school graduates in his domain. Perhaps, the new graduates are better off in Iraq or Afghanistan. The Defense Department is trying to market military service to 16- and 17-year-olds with the hope that high-school seniors will sign up for the military upon graduation.

The Defense Department is working with a private marketing company to create a database of high-school and college students. The Defense Department is trying to identify potential recruits by getting information such as birth dates, Social Security numbers, e-mail addresses, grade-point averages, ethnicity and subjects the students are studying.

It has some information already on potential recruits through the No Child Left Behind Act. Military recruiters have called students' homes trying to find 18-year-olds to join the armed forces.

Last time anyone looked, basic training was a lot tougher than any NBA training camp. Qualifying to become an Army Ranger is harder than making the Orlando Magic and sitting on the bench at 18.

The United States is sending 18-year-olds into harm's way. Stern is banishing 18-year-olds from his league. Maybe Stern is trying to shield them from the Knicks City Dancers or the Lakers Cheerleaders. He said it does not send a good message that his league's scouts are in high-school gyms looking at players. One has to wonder what Stern thinks about the Defense Department's recruiting techniques.

What is even more baffling is how NBA-beat writers and sports-radio talk-show hosts have bought into Stern's argument, and how NBA basketball will benefit from not having 18-year-olds in a 30-team league. Basketball, both on the college and NBA level, is fluff entertainment, that's all. Yes, billions of dollars flow into the industry, but it's not the real world.

Somehow, all of us have allowed sports to get out of hand. Years ago, Howard Cosell told this reporter and anyone else within earshot, "Sports is out of whack." Sports is even more out of whack now than when Cosell uttered the phrase back in the late 1980s.

Stern is wrong in barring 18-year-olds from his private business that depends heavily on government largesse and approval.

Stern is the keeper of fluff entertainment. How can he welcome an 18-year-old into his league this year, and then deprive another one of the same chance the next? Is an 18-year-old old enough to serve his country, but not old enough to play basketball?

There is something very wrong with that picture.

Endorsement/Sponsorship

Endorsement Dollars Driving the Push for Clean Athletes
Metro, June 12, 2004

Track and field's Marion Jones and cycling's Lance Armstrong have come out swinging daring people to prove that they are using performance-enhancing drugs or that they are blood doping.

But here is a bigger question for those who are accusing Jones, Armstrong and a host of others of using performance-enhancing drugs. Do you care about the athlete's health or do you care about the potential loss of advertising dollars and tickets sales from a drug scandal?

Jones says she is clean. She also wants a public hearing into her alleged performance enhancing drug use, and wants to compete in this year's Olympics (despite failing to qualify for the 100-meter dash, she has several more chances to qualify for other events).

Armstrong wants to put to rest rumors of doping accusations. But if the strong fan support we have seen in baseball is any guide, the public really doesn't care if athletes are taking performance-enhancing drugs.

So who is really bothered by the allegations that athletes are using drugs to give them an edge in competition? It seemed President Bush and his advisers are. The President spent two minutes of his State of the Union speech addressing steroid usage.

Congress got into the act and five members of the House introduced legislation that would ban steroid use. There was one problem with the legislation. Steroid possession in the United States is illegal unless prescribed by a doctor.

As recently as June 18, Senator John Mc Cain (R-Ariz.), chairman of the Senate Commerce Committee, said he felt Jones should pursue her complaints with the US Anti-Doping Agency, not the Senate, since his committee isn't a court of law or arbitration panel. So much for straight talk from Mc Cain.

Major League Baseball Commissioner Bud Selig was pushing for stronger steroid testing, but once the season got underway, the issue faded into the background.

So why are people like Jones and Armstrong fighting so hard to protect their images? It may have a lot to do with endorsements and the millions upon millions of dollars that are out there for sports organizations and athletes and nothing to do with health.

International Olympic Committee member and Chairman of the World Anti-Doping Agency Richard Pound of Canada is one of the few people who claims he is concerned with health issues. But how many other people share Pound's stated "concern" about the health of athletes?

Are sports organizations really concerned about the health and welfare of athletes or are they worried about drug scandals sullying their images and their marketing abilities? Based on how sports treats its athletes once their marketability is gone and they no longer can sell merchandise, it appears a clean image is far more important than health issues.

Gambling Gets Double Standard

Metro [Philly], July 22, 2004

Once again, sports owners are using a double standard when it comes to gambling and their businesses. Pennsylvania has legalized slot machine gambling at race tracks around the state. Although "Major League Sports" has pretty much accepted that gambling has been legitimized through casinos, state lotteries and off-track betting offices, the National Football League has a problem with Steelers running back Jerome Bettis who is involved in a development project in Pittsburgh that could feature slots.

Bettis may have violated some NFL bylaw that allows teams to accept advertising revenue from racetracks and state lotteries but prohibits players or coaches from appearing in the gambling ads. It is kind of strange in that Bettis is an employee of the Rooney family whose patriarch Art Rooney, Sr. allegedly founded the Steelers in 1933 with an endowment provided by the winnings on a bet from a horse race. Bettis may have violated NFL rules by being a spokesman for his group and lobbying Harrisburg lawmakers, but the Rooney family can own New York's floundering Yonkers Raceway, which will get a major boost from slot machines in 2005, and a Florida dog track.

NHL Commissioner Gary Bettman has no problem with the recently passed legislation if it helps bring Mario Lemieux and his Pittsburgh Penguins ownership a new arena by 2007. The Penguins could be skating in a new facility thanks to a West Virginia developer Ted Arneault who hopes to secure a racetrack license in Pittsburgh and build a track complete with slots. Should Arneault get the license, he has promised to deliver $60 million of the slots money to Lemieux and his ownership group as a partial payment for the new arena.

Bettman should have no complaints about the Pennsylvania slot machine legislation. The NHL long ago dropped its anti-gambling stance and accepted money from the Alberta Provincial Hockey Lottery that put money into the Calgary Flames and Edmonton Oilers owners' pockets. Alberta decided to share lottery "proceeds" to keep those two teams financially competitive with some of the NHL's weaker and small fiscal market franchises.

Bettman has also been pushing other provinces to share their hockey lottery monies with NHL teams. As long as there is no sports book, Bettman is fine with gambling.

Sports, including Major League Baseball, which has kept Pete Rose sidelined because of gambling, takes advertising dollars from casinos, racetracks and other gambling forms, so that is why the Bettis situation is so baffling.

The NFL had no problem when Cleveland Browns owner Art Modell decided in fall 1995 to move his team to Baltimore and to a stadium that was being built with the proceeds from the Maryland State Lottery.

Steelers president Art Rooney II is concerned that slots could lead to illegal sports betting.

If Rooney and his cohorts are so concerned, they should not accept advertising from casinos and lotteries and the Ravens new ownership should offer to pay the debt on their facility instead of using Maryland lottery monies.

Show Them the Money / Why Athletes Sit on the Political Bench
Orlando Sentinel, October 6, 2004

Bruce Springsteen is rockin' on the highly visible and politically charged Vote For Change concert tour, which includes a stop in Orlando on Friday, in sports arenas in so-called swing states such as Florida. But don't expect to see any athletes sharing the stage with the musician. That would cause too many problems for athletes who don't get too involved with either social or political issues because it's not good for their careers or business.

Entertainers don't mind speaking out, as it's part of a long tradition of being expressive. Athletes are just supposed to shut up and play.

Athletes love to compare themselves to entertainers, and both Democrats and Republicans regularly court "NASCAR dads" and "soccer moms," but athletes are not very politically active because they know they can lose their jobs and their endorsements for voicing their views. Neither their owners nor the fans want to know their opinions any way.

Springsteen, who will be joined at various arenas by Babyface, Jackson Browne, Bright Eyes, Dave Matthews Band, Death Cab for Cutie, the Dixie Chicks, John Fogerty, Ben Harper, Jurassic 5, Keb' Mo', John Mellencamp, My Morning Jacket, Pearl Jam, Bonnie Raitt, R.E.M., James Taylor and the E Street Band, will be urging his audience to vote for John Kerry in the November presidential election.

Because of the possible career consequences, professional athletes don't stage protests over social issues. They become controversial only because of inane on-field antics or maybe because they are flashy or say something about a team or an opponent. They don't cause problems by questioning President George W. Bush's Iraq policies, as Toronto Blue Jays baseball player Carlos Delgado did earlier his summer, or complain about the after-effects of the U.S. Navy's usage of the island of Vieques in Puerto Rico as Delgado also did earlier this summer.

Delgado would have been a good fit for Springsteen's concert tour but would be lonely if he was looking for the company of fellow players. He was the only one to take a public anti-war stand, and Delgado's teammate Greg Zaun is apparently no fan of Delgado or the Dixie Chicks or entertainers who speak their minds.

"There's a lot of idiot liberals in the entertainment industry," Zaun was quoted when asked about the Dixie Chicks singer Natalie Maines, who, before the start of the Iraq war, told a London concert crowd, "Just so you know, we're ashamed the president of the United States is from Texas."

Athletes, from an early age, are encouraged by all sorts of handlers to stay mute. It's part of the athlete's culture.

Don't say anything.

Zaun's remark, in itself, was somewhat interesting, because players are supposed to be seen and not heard. There are three reasons that athletes are like children in that they should be seen and not heard.

Marketing. Career. And the brainwashing.

It is far better for Michael Jordan to select "hand-picked" athletes like Derek Jeter for his Jordan fashion line than talk about Nike sweatshops or make an endorsement in a political contest, as he could have in 1996 when the North Carolina Senate race pitted the incumbent Jesse Helms against Democrat Harvey Gantt. Jordan explained it away simply by saying, "Republicans buy sneakers, too."

Look what happened to Muhammad Ali. In 1967, Ali refused to be inducted into the U.S. military and subsequently lost not only his title but also his livelihood and risked prison time for refusing military service as a protest over the Vietnam War. Ali gave up more than three years of his career.

Sports is unforgiving when someone is judged to be on the "wrong" side of the issue.

No athlete, other than Delgado, has taken the stand that Manhattan College women's basketball player Toni Smith did during her senior year in 2003. She simply turned away from the United States flag during the playing of the national anthem prior to her games at the Manhattanville College campus in Purchase, N.Y. Smith never did fully explain her decision, but that didn't stop right-wing radio talk-show hosts and sports commentators from condemning her or saying that sports and politics should never collide.

Smith is a great example as to why athletes stay silent. There is too much pressure on them and too much money for them to voice an opinion.

So when Springsteen and his fellow musicians come through Orlando, don't expect many Magic players or other athletes to be up on stage with him and the others. Athletes know their place is to be seen and not heard if they want to keep playing and selling T-shirts and sneakers.

Labor

Why Contraction Isn't Necessarily a Solution
A Syndicated Piece, June 1, 2001

Is Bud Selig damaging Major League Baseball's credibility by talking about contraction? Selig is sounding more like a tough talking CEO threatening to lay off 10 percent of his workforce than a Sports Commissioner selling his game to fans. Selig is leaving the option of dropping two to four economically failing teams on the table.

Selig may be talking like a CEO but Baseball's problem isn't necessarily about not having enough money. Baseball's problem is the distribution of money among its 30 individual entities. It has become a business of financially fit franchises with hefty revenues streams, (the New York Yankees) and teams with poor revenue streams, (the Montreal Expos) and the disparity starts on the team level with a wide variation of local TV contracts.

The easiest thing to do is talk about folding franchises; the hardest thing to do is actually putting teams out of business. To start, Major League Baseball needs an even number of franchises to showcase its product, which are games, and Selig and his fellow owners would have to buy out either two or four teams. Is there a mechanism to do that currently in place? The answer is no. Baseball last folded Major League teams in the 19th century.

In fact, the last time a "Major League" sport disbanded a franchise was in 1978 when the National Hockey League merged the Cleveland Barons and Minnesota North Stars. The North Stars ownership took over the Barons' player contracts and Cleveland no longer had a team.

Baseball has contracts in place with municipalities in St. Petersburg and Minneapolis that would need to be bought out, if Selig and his fellow owners decide to pull the plug on the Tampa Bay Devil Rays and the Minnesota Twins. How much would municipalities, which built stadiums with public funding and are paying off bonds on the facilities, want as a settlement?

Selig and his fellow owners would have to buy back the franchises from those owners as well. How much would they pay to end a team?

How much would Carl Polhad want in Minnesota? How much would the Schott-Hoffman partnership in Oakland want? How much would Jeffrey Loria in Montreal want? How much would John Henry in South Florida want? How much would the Tampa Bay partners want?

Would Selig and his fellow owners run afoul of the United States Congress? The 1993 expansion to Denver and South Florida partly came about because Senators Tim Wirth of Colorado and Connie Mack of Florida were putting heat on Baseball to expand or risk losing the sport's anti-trust exemption.

The 1998 expansion to St. Petersburg and Phoenix came about after Phoenix area residents approved the building of a baseball park, but the money package had an expiration date in April 1995. If Major League Baseball did not expand or move a franchise to Phoenix by then, the stadium would not be built.

Baseball has been a partner with taxpayers and cities for years and years. The industry took sweetheart leases and put teams into cities that might not have the wherewithal to support an industry that requires about 400,000 people attending games five to eight times a year.

There is also a trickle down effect on Minor League Baseball. As a result of the 1990 agreement between Major League Owners and Minor League Operators, cities across the country invest millions upon millions of dollars to either build new facilities or upgrade stadiums to Major League Baseball specifications. With Major League Baseball adding four teams in the 1990s, Triple AAA and Double AA leagues also added four teams each, and Single A baseball also added teams.

If Selig and his fellow owners decide to lop off two or four teams, so will the minor leagues. Will cities and municipalities that built new facilities in good faith for minor league baseball expansion sit back idly as those areas lose Triple A and Double A status?

There are also television and radio agreements that would be broken in the areas that would lose teams, and would Los Angeles Dodgers owner and FOX owner Ruppert Murdoch and ESPN ask to renegotiate national TV deals with Major League Baseball if there were fewer markets? Would national sponsors and partners pull out of agreements with Major League Baseball with fewer teams?

There is another problem with contraction. There are areas that think they could make great baseball cities. Portland, Oregon, Santa Clara and Washington/Northern Virginia all want to make pitches for teams. Portland is eyeing whatever team becomes available. Santa Clara would like to entice the Oakland A's to move about 50 miles south into the South Bay, Washington and Northern Virginia have different groups ready to bring Baseball back to the Beltway. Why fold teams if someone else wants to take a chance?

Major League Baseball would cut about eight percent of its on field workforce dropping two teams or 50 players. Baseball would also eliminate entire business and sales staffs, general managers, farm directors, scouts, trainers, assistant trainers, equipment managers, clubhouse attendants, managers and coaches. On the minor league level, cutbacks would include a dozen managers, about 30 coaches, trainers, and probably about 250 players.

Selig and his fellow owners have another series of questions that need to be answered. If contraction is on the table, why hasn't Selig talked to the Players Association Executive Director Donald Fehr or the rank and file members of the Players Association about the possibility of cutting back two to four teams? Is Selig using the idea of contraction as a negotiating tool? The present Collective Bargaining Agreement is up on October 31 and does Major League Baseball plan to use the threat of eliminating two to four teams as leverage to get something from the Players Association?

By publicly talking about contraction is Bud Selig damaging the Baseball industry?

Baseball Agreement Strikes Out Steinbrenner
Newsday, New York, September 13, 2002

George Steinbrenner wasn't among those baseball fans who were ecstatic that the owners and players had come up with a new collective bargaining agreement, preventing a strike. The Yankee owner knows that the new four-year deal that the owners approved is not only bad for him but also for all New Yorkers, Yankee fans and non-baseball fans.

Baseball owners couldn't beat Steinbrenner on the field, so they devised a scheme to beat him in the corporate boardroom. The players and owners acted in their own best interests. But no one acted in our best interests. And that's too bad, because people from our area will pay to prop up poorly run baseball teams in other cities.

For selfish reasons, Steinbrenner voted no because the new deal could cost him millions. But he could also have rejected it to protect his partners, YES Network subscribers and luxury-box and club-seats season ticket holders, and here's why:

Just about all New York-area cable subscribers (except, of course, Cablevision customers) are paying the Yankees directly for the right to have their games cablecast and that adds up to millions of dollars. The Yankees charge top dollar for their limited number of luxury boxes and special high-end seating. What the owners wanted to do—and accomplished with the players' help—was to penalize the Yankees for having the ability to generate millions of dollars more than the rest of them.

On top of that, somehow, someone in the owners' negotiating team figured out that a superstar player like Derek Jeter is a luxury, not just a mere baseball player. So, under the new agreement, Steinbrenner will be fined if he chooses to pay his players more than what Commissioner (and the father of the present Milwaukee Brewers owner) Bud Selig and his merry band of baseball barons have decided is a fair limit for salaries.

What may be fair to Selig and his owners isn't very fair to those who invest a great deal of money into the Yankees and expect a high rate of return: a pennant winner. In the new world order of baseball, superiority may no longer be the standard of excellence. Talented players will become luxuries. Mediocrity will be rewarded.

Selig and his fellow owners can do whatever they please because they are like an oil cartel. Don't forget that Major League Baseball has the Supreme Court's seal of approval to operate as a monopoly, thanks to Chief Justice Oliver Wendell Holmes' 1922 decision that baseball is a sport, not a business.

In 2002, the owners got help from the players. The owners wanted to take Steinbrenner's money, which is really the cable subscribers' dough along with luxury-box and club-seating receipts, and redistribute it to so-called needy franchises like Walt Disney's Anaheim Angels or the Toronto Blue Jays, whose president Paul Godfrey has already said he plans to use his revenue-share payment to pay off Blue Jay debts. The team claims it lost $50 million in 2001. Needy franchise owners don't have to use the money to recruit veteran players. If, say, Minnesota Twins owner Carl Pohlad, one of the richest men on the planet, decides to keep the money, he can.

All of this should be very troubling to city officials who are giving Steinbrenner and Mets owner Fred Wilpon about $50 million over the next five years to do research and planning for a new Yankee Stadium and a new Shea Stadium somewhere down the road. With the city experiencing a $5-billion shortfall, it seems wrong even to have new stadium plans on the drawing board, but the city does.

Baseball's increased revenue sharing becomes a serious problem for Bloomberg and the city, should former Mayor Rudolph Giuliani's shelved plans for two new baseball venues become a reality. Under Giuliani's old proposal, the city and state would have paid the lion's share of the cost of the two facilities through various tax plans. Both baseball and non-baseball fans would have picked up the costs whether they approve of the plan or not.

Giuliani said that without new stadiums to generate more revenue, both New York teams would be unable to compete with other teams in the future. He wanted new venues so the Mets and Yankees could sell many more luxury boxes and club seats.

The baseball agreement has proved Giuliani wrong. We don't need new publicly funded stadiums. The Yankees have more than enough money to compete. They have so much that they have to "share" some $50 million or so annually, which is why the well-known attorney David Boies has been put on retainer, just in case Steinbrenner wants to sue baseball. Boies, of course, sued Microsoft and won.

Reckless Spending Is at the Root of the NHL's Labor Woes

Metro, New York Edition, September 7, 2004

There is just one major issue that needs to be resolved in the labor talks between the National Hockey League owners and the National Hockey League Players Association.

The owners and their lead negotiator, Commissioner Gary Bettman, want the players to come up with a mechanism to protect them from overspending. It's really that simple.

The owners want a salary cap and to limit their spending, and want the players union's blessing. NHL owners have jacked up salaries, not the players. The owners are responsible for their fiscal woes, not the players, yet the owners don't want to take responsibility for the irresponsible spending on players salaries which they contend is seriously threatening the future of the National Hockey League.

The NHL produced a study by Arthur Levitt, the longest-serving chair of the US Securities and Exchange Commission and former chairman of the American Stock Exchange, which contended that its 30 teams had lost a collective $273 million in 2002–03. Levitt contended that the NHL is a poor investment yet people are still buying NHL franchises and cities like Kansas City and Winnipeg want back into the league. The New Jersey Devils were just sold to Jeffrey Vanderbeek.

Just how bad are the finances? That's a tough question to answer. There are so many levels of income that need to be considered. For example what is the true value of the Rangers' cable TV package and does the Garden factor that into the Rangers' bottom line or the Garden's overall bottom line?

The players have an unlikely ally in their corner in this battle. Former NHL President John Ziegler. Ziegler has pointed the finger of blame directly at the owners who, he said, were outmaneuvered in individual player contract negotiations by agents and that caused players' salaries to skyrocket.

According to Ziegler, who was the NHL's President between 1977 and 1992, agents would use Wayne Gretzky as the standard. If Gretzky scored 92 goals and their client scored 23, then their client is clearly 25 percent as good as Gretzky and therefore should get a quarter of Gretzky's salary, which was the highest in the league in the 1980s and 90s.

The owner would agree and grab that 23-goal scorer at a higher price. Then a different owner, not to be outdone, would sign someone else's 23-goal scorer at a slightly higher salary, ratcheting up player costs.

The worst offenders were the New York Rangers who would sign older players past their primes to enormous contracts.

NHL owners are now asking their employees to police themselves and that is why contract talks are apparently going nowhere and why National Hockey League owners could lockout their players next week.

On surface, MLB Rolling; Dig Deeper and Conditions Dire

Metro, September 20, 2004

Perceived perception.

Major League Baseball has regained the perceived perception from sportswriters, sports radio talk show hosts and TV sports barkers that it is hot again.

Yes, attendance is up and mlb.com is getting record views. But TV ratings are low, the game is widely unpopular among minorities and at least four franchises have serious stadium problems.

But people are more interested in perception than reality and that seems to hold true in Bud Selig's case.

The reality is that no one really wants to take the Montreal Expos off of Selig and his 29 fellow owners hands. The reality is that the Florida Marlins, Minnesota Twins and the Oakland Athletes remain candidates for extinction. The reality is that Selig's family is trying to sell the Brewers after it was revealed that Selig might not have been above board in his negotiations with Wisconsin in getting a new stadium built in Milwaukee.

Selig was named as a defendant in a complaint filed under the RICO act that alleges a conspiracy on the part of Jeffrey Loria and Major League Baseball to defraud the Canadian partners in the Expos of their share in the major league franchise and to destroy baseball in Montreal. That case is now before the American Arbitration Association in New York after a Florida judge ordered arbitration to settle the matter. The arbitrators' decision may come down sometime during October.

Meanwhile it looks more and more as if the Expos will be returning to Montreal in 2005 for a third lame duck season. Selig and his administration had hopes of getting a stadium built somewhere and then selling the Expos but hasn't happened. Baseball has received setbacks in Washington, DC and Northern Virginia in its effort to relocate the Expos into that market.

Last Tuesday, Washingtonians elected three anti-stadium city council candidates. In Virginia, the state isn't sure if it wants to use moral obligation bonds to back a stadium.

The Expos situation is just one of the industry's problems. There still remains a lack of trust between the players and owners in contract negotiations. Some agents think the owners have colluded in keeping salaries down, just like Selig and his fellow owners did in the 1980s, but they have a hard time proving it while George Steinbrenner is willing to pay top dollar for talent.

Bud Selig is being judged on perceived perception and that is a good thing if you consider the reality.

Kerry Could Spark NHL Labor Peace
Metro, October 28, 2004

Coincidence or not, the National Hockey League Players Association will be meeting in Toronto to discuss the next steps in their battle to get a new Collective Bargaining Agreement with NHL owners on Election Day.

The coincidence is this. The NHLPA is meeting at the very time that American voters are deciding on who should be president and that vote may have a major ramification on the NHL Lockout.

Some facts here: the NHL and the NHLPA have not met since September 9. It appears the talks have reached an impasse yet the NHLPA has not filed any grievances at this point with the National Labor Relations Board (NLRB) charging that the NHL has not bargained in good faith.

Could Kerry help matters?

There could be a reason for this. President George W. Bush has been appointing pro-business people to the National Labor Relations Board and to the justice system.

The NHLPA may just wait to see if John Kerry is elected President and because Kerry is both a Democrat and a friend of labor unions, the anticipation is that Kerry would appoint people to the NRLB who would be more sympathetic to the plight of organized labor. If Kerry wins, the NHLPA could be very quick to file a complaint.

The NLRB was instrumental in ending the 1994–95 Major League Baseball strike. Once a judge got involved, both sides immediately got back to the bargaining table to hammer out a deal.

The National Hockey League has settled its past two labor disputes in 1992 and 1994–95 without "outside" help. The National Basketball Association also ended it labor dispute without "outside" assistance.

Whether that is the case this time could depend on the outcome of Tuesday's election.

NBA Headed Toward Lockout of Its Own?

MSNBC.com, December 3, 2004

National Basketball Association fans across the country, in Canada and around the world should take a long look at what is going on in the National Hockey League lockout because the odds are pretty good that basketball fans will be witnessing an NBA work stoppage at this time next year. And it has nothing to do with the Pistons–Pacers brawl in Auburn Hills, Mich.

It's all about money.

Like NHL owners, NBA owners want to change their business model and get even more cost certainty and tighten budgets. They want their teams to be more profitable and they are going to ask the players to agree to what they want and if the players don't, it's too bad.

The gates will be locked and the workers outside. The players will be punished unless they agree to a new collective bargaining agreement for owners' mismanagement and financial mistakes.

The players' salaries, which were approved by owners, have to come down.

It's that simple. If there are no games, too bad for the owners, too bad for the fans. The fans always come back anyway besides that's what they live for, the games. They won't find other things to do. Just look at the 1994–95 baseball strike and how many fans said they would never come back. Or the 1992 NHL strike or the 1994–95 NHL lockout or the 1998–99 NBA lockout.

The fans came back.

The NBA could have locked out its players this season, but decided to play through. Both NHL and the NBA owners have run out of places to find new money.

The NHL, according to one-time San Jose Sharks owner George Gund, got enough network TV money to buy only a third line left wing. But the new NHL-NBC television deal won't even bring in that money. (NBC is a partner in the joint venture that runs NBCSports.com)

The NBA took a hit when NBC decided it could not afford paying the kind of money the NBA sought. The NBA did in the end get a nice deal with Turner Sports and Disney, but for the most part, the league has disappeared from network television.

That is spelling trouble for David Stern and his 30 owners. Sports are at the crossroads. The NFL continues to run as a well-oiled machine with new TV contracts already signed for 2006 and beyond.

But the other Big 3—the NHL, the NBA and Major League Baseball—are in trouble because they are tapped out when it comes to new revenue streams.

Ticket prices are very high, too high for the average person to attend more than a handful of games. All the satellite TV technologies are in place; no one is inventing cable TV or satellite TV type products that will bring additional money into owner's pockets.

The owners are looking to fix what they perceive is a cash flow problem in the NHL. The league contends too many teams are bringing in too few dollars to meet costs. Although in some instances it's hard to tell just what is real and what isn't because teams are part of cable companies and those companies may not be paying fair market price for cable TV rights, thus depressing the bottom line.

The NBA has better TV contracts than the NHL, but the owners want to tighten the salary cap by shortening guaranteed contracts and raising the luxury tax to make it harder for free agents to change teams. The NBA Players Association Executive Director Billy Hunter will never go for that, which could mean that the NBA will join the NHL in preventing their players from performing in 2005. The NHL owners seem willing to stay out for as long as they can gain what they want from the players and if that takes until 2006, they don't seem to mind.

NHL owners would rather sit out than sign a bad collective bargaining agreement.

Major League Baseball owners are watching the hockey lockout and will more than likely study the NBA talks waiting for their turn at the negotiating table. They, like their comrades in the NHL and the NBA, would like to bring down salaries.

These are troubling times for sports fans. The owners are determined to regain control of players' salaries. In doing so, they may burn down the village and scorch the earth to get their way.

The question after they do all of that is whether or not people will care enough to watch them rebuild their sports league or if the fans will have found something else to do with their time. The owners are betting they will come back.

Selig Can't Be Judge, Jury, Executioner
MSNBC.com, December 5, 2004

Major League Baseball has a major credibility problem, but its steroid scandal is small potatoes in the overall scheme of day-to-day life in the United States. Someone violated and compromised the judicial system by leaking grand jury testimony to a San Francisco newspaper, and that's a far bigger problem than if Jason Giambi and Barry Bonds used steroids.

Giambi and Bonds were answering questions in secrecy and that testimony was supposed to be sealed. That's a major breach and Attorney General John Ashcroft or his successor needs to address that breach.

As far as baseball goes, steroid usage is illegal unless a physician prescribes it. Apparently Giambi and Bonds got their steroids from a trainer, but that will eventually be decided by the judicial system. That is where baseball needs to start its probe of steroid use in the sport.

Both Giambi and Bonds did something illegal.

Whether or not Bonds, Giambi and others have "tainted" the game in the same manner that say Pete Rose did when he allegedly bet on baseball is uncertain. But by using steroids, they have violated U.S. law, although they are no different than the average guy or woman who uses steroids at the local gym to build up their bodies or high school athletes who take illegal drugs to perform better and attract college or pro offers.

That is the reality of steroid use in sports, from high school to the pros. It exists no matter how many people deny it.

Meanwhile, can Commissioner Bud Selig or New York Yankees owner George Steinbrenner be credible judges in handing out penalties to Bonds, Giambi and possibly others who testified in the BALCO case? Selig must hire an independent panel to investigate the BALCO issues. He also must disqualify himself because he was part of the group of owners who were found guilty by an arbitrator for colluding and depressing salaries illegally following the 1985, 1986 and 1987 seasons.

Selig was also one of the 28 owners who were found guilty of bad faith bargaining in the 1994–95 baseball strike. Steinbrenner was a convicted felon for giving illegal contributions to Richard Nixon's 1972 presidential campaign and was twice suspended from the game. Steinbrenner was pardoned in 1989 by President Reagan in one of his final official acts in office.

After the *San Francisco Chronicle* broke the Giambi testimony, Selig said, "I've been saying for many months: I instituted a very, very tough program in the minor leagues on steroids in 2001. We need to have that program at the major league level. We're going to leave no stone unturned until we have that policy in place by spring training 2005."

While Selig has been talking tough, there seems to be a failure in the recognition that steroid use is illegal.

There is a failure of recognition from both the owners' side and the players association side. Both sides are using steroids as a bargaining issue in the upcoming collective bargaining talks. The problem is fueled by both sides knowing that baseball fans really don't care whether players take the juice or not and are more concerned about who hit the ball over the fence and how far it went. Tape measure homeruns are a selling point, a television highlight that might sell tickets to individual fans, amuse luxury box and club seat patrons. Baseball is big business and doesn't seem to care much about its performers' health no matter what lip service Selig and the players association gives to the steroid/human growth hormone problem.

Sports has a poster boy for what happens when someone takes steroids. One time Denver Broncos, Cleveland Browns and Los Angeles Raiders defensive lineman Lyle Alzado died on May 14, 1992 at the age of 43 from brain cancer.

Alzado, before his death, said he suffered from a rare lymphoma of the central nervous system which he claimed was caused by his extensive use of anabolic steroids including Dianabol.

"I started taking anabolic steroids in 1969 and never stopped. It was addicting, mentally addicting. Now I'm sick, and I'm scared… I became very violent on the field and off it. I did things only crazy people do," he recalled. "Once a guy sideswiped my car and I beat the hell out of him. Now look at me. My hair's gone, I wobble when I walk and have to hold on to someone for support, and I have trouble remembering things."

Alzado's story should have been repeated countless times in all football, baseball, basketball, hockey and sports circles. Instead, newer forms of steroids and other human growth hormones have been developed since his death and so have masks to hide its usage. Alzado's tale did nothing to stop Ken Caminiti who admitted using steroids during 1996 when he was the National League's most valuable player.

Jose Canseco was dismissed by sportswriters when he planned to write a tell all book including who used steroids. Canseco may have been a character, but there seems to be something worth investigating.

Maybe baseball and the union don't want to know and are hiding their heads in the sand because they know fans don't care except for how far the ball was hit. That's why baseball cannot internally do a steroid investigation and needs to turn outward and hire an independent board to see just how widespread a problem steroids really are in the industry.

Silence About NHL Lockout is Deafening

NBCSports.com, January 18, 2005

One of the more fascinating aspects of the National Hockey League's lockout is how quiet politicians, civic leaders and labor unions have been as the dispute drags on.

The NHL owners began their lockout last spring, when both individual teams and owners began firing front office employees preparing for the Sept. 15 lockout. At that time, there was no talk about how people were losing their jobs from politicians, who were offering any solution that came into their head to solve baseball's steroid problem. There has been a deafening silence from mayors, including New York's Michael Bloomberg, Los Angeles' Jim Hahn, Chicago's Richard Daley, Philadelphia's James Street and their smaller NHL city counterparts, about the lockout, which is entering its fifth month.

Mayors and governors also produce various studies and show all types of positive numbers and economic growth patterns to justify municipal spending to build multi-million-dollar stadiums and arenas for teams and leagues. So it should follow that the 24 cities in the U.S., which host NHL teams, have lost money from the lockout. Yet where is the outrage from political leaders?

U.S. Senator John McCain threatened to punish the Major League Baseball Players Association and impose steroid testing on baseball players if they and the baseball owners didn't come up with a steroid-testing plan. The Arizona Republican claimed he and his colleagues in Congress could impose mandatory testing on the players, because Major League Baseball fell under his purview as interstate commerce.

Under that thinking, McCain should be imposing his considerable weight and influence to finding a solution for the NHL. But McCain has been mute on the lockout, despite the fact that the NHL's Coyotes are in Glendale, Ariz., and Glendale Arena employees and area businesses have lost money because no games have been played.

Business and union leaders have said even less. As part of the argument for bringing in a franchise or building a new arena, team owners or politicians always recruit business leaders to tout the benefits of having a franchise. Business leaders parrot the line of politicians who claim that sports teams and arenas/stadiums are economic linchpins that create jobs, business opportunities and a good feeling among the area's population who root, root, root for the home team. Why are those business leaders so mute?

Why are union leaders so quiet? In some NHL cities, union members are losing money because there are no games. Yet no one from the AFL-CIO or other trade unions has said a word about the lockout.

Does anyone except for some scattered fans really care? If the NHL or sports in general are economic linchpins, why is there no outside pressure from the White House and the Bush administration to end this dispute?

What is even more baffling is that Canadian Prime Minister Paul Martin has not put enormous pressure on the owners and players to get the sides together at his Ottawa offices as President Bill Clinton did in early 1995 after the Major League Baseball Players Association went on strike.

"There's only a role for Ottawa if the parties want it," Martin told CBC television in December. "There's not a role for Ottawa if Ottawa simply goes in there and says to either the players' association or the owners, 'Look now, here we come.'"

Hockey may not attract an across the board fan base, but if you look strictly at TV numbers, its audience is not much smaller than Major League Baseball or the NBA, and the league is a multi-billion dollar industry. It will be interesting to see the general reaction of politicians, business and labor leaders if the NBA locks out its players July 1, and in two years when the baseball owners and players will be embroiled in a labor negotiations. Will there be action or just silence?

Is the NHL a Trendsetter?
Washington Examiner, February 3, 2005

Just in case you haven't noticed, there is a seismic shift taking place in the sports world and its aftershocks may be extraordinary. People better get used to long work stoppages in sports because of a fight over money.

The five-month old National Hockey League lockout has ushered in a new age of sports reality and sports economics. Owners have decided to flex their collective muscle and drive down salaries and the NHL is the first on line. The National Basketball Association could lockout its players next July 1 and Major League Baseball may do the same in 2007.

The National Football League has an owner-friendly salary cap system and is also at the crossroads. The players want changes in the system and it already has become a sticking point in preliminary collective bargaining negotiations.

The NHL lockout was caused by owners who could not say "No" to players' financial demands. Now the owners want the players to protect them from making bad financial decisions. If NHL Commissioner Gary Bettman doesn't get a salary cap, Edmonton's owners are ready to suspend operations and other owners may declare bankruptcy.

In the 1990s, as the salaries increased, the owners were able to cover the costs with national TV deals, expansion fees (the NHL went from 21 to 30 teams), a rise in ticket prices, new buildings opening with more luxury boxes and club seats and monies from new technologies like cable and satellite TV.

In 2004, all of that enhanced revenue was gone. Ticket prices are too high for the average person. NHL owners want cost certainty because their revenues aren't going up as quickly as the players' salaries are.

But does cost certainty work?

Apparently it doesn't in the NBA. In 1999, after an owners' lockout, the players and owners came up with a new revenue sharing system, which is not working as well as Commissioner David Stern and his owners want. Part of the problem was caused by a loss of a significant chunk of cash from TV rights as the present deal is worth far less than the previous deal. Stern will push to limit guaranteed contracts down and raise the luxury tax as a way to control costs. That push will lead to a July 1 lockout.

If Major League Baseball is played in 2007, it may depend on the kind of deal that the hockey players accept. Major League Baseball owners have been handing out huge contracts this off-season and it has caught the eye of Pittsburgh Pirates owner Kevin McClatchy. McClatchy is blaming his fellow owners, not the players, for overspending. That is why McClatchy is rooting for the NHL. An NHL owners' victory may go a long way in determining just how far baseball owners are willing to go in an effort to achieve their own cost certainty. The NHL may be the least watched of the four major sports, but its lockout will have major ramifications on the other three.

NHL: Replacing a Lost Season?
The Washington Examiner, April 18, 2005

The next set of steps in the National Hockey League lockout will be climbed this week when NHL owners will talk amongst themselves and more than likely be reopening their businesses on Wednesday. But in what kind of shape is the shuttered business that hasn't operated in about 10 months?

The owners and players are still haggling over a new Collective Bargaining Agreement. The owners can certainly ride out a lockout, but can the players continue not collecting over a billion dollars in salaries?

Very little has been said about individual players who have lost millions of dollars with no chance of making back that money. Association members have received a monthly stipend with monies ranging from $5,000–10,000.

On top of that, there is a turnover of about 15 percent of players annually, which means about 15 percent of the present National Hockey League Players Association membership will never see another NHL check.

The players' side may be hurting and that may present an opening for the owners, although most of the players have said very little about losing over a billion dollars collectively in salaries.

If there is a Collective Bargaining Agreement in place by Wednesday, the league will rehire marketing and public relations specialists to help sell the NHL brand name and hope to have a baseball style economic surge.

But if there is no Collective Bargaining Agreement in place, and there is no reason to believe that a new CBA will be finalized by Wednesday, expect to see a good number of American-born ECHL, United Hockey League and Central Hockey League players along with foreign born players who are permitted to work in the United States wearing NHL uniforms with some NHL players joining them next season.

The idea of replacement players has been kicked around for a while and it is unclear if Toronto, Ottawa, Montreal and Vancouver can ever ice teams because of Canadian labor laws regarding replacement workers during a lockout

Should NHL owners decide to go ahead with replacements, there will be a flurry of legal briefs filed. The owners have already filed two complaints with the National Labor Relations Board accusing the league's players' association of threatening to decertify agents that represent replacement players and the league filed an unfair labor practice charge, accusing the union of violating its members' rights by asking players to repay their lockout stipend if they choose to become replacement players.

If the owners go ahead with replacements, the players will file a grievance with the NRLB. In 1995, the Major League Baseball strike ended after a series of legal maneuvering. The NFL ended over 20 years of legal fights with its players in 1993 when Judge David Doty pressured both sides into signing an agreement.

The NHL is promising to deliver a season in 2005–06 but league owners will find out that it is easier to promise games than it is to stage them without a Collective Bargaining Agreement in place.

Events

This Race Will Get Us Moving Again
Newsday, New York City Edition, October 11, 2001

Sure, there are a few people running for office today but in a month the city will be filled with thousands of runners—and their race could be the emotional and economic starting point of our road to recovery.

The New York City Marathon could do more for the city's morale and its coffers than any Yankees playoff game, no offense Bronx Bombers. This event is probably much more important to our fiscal health than getting the 2012 Summer Olympics, let alone the 2002 Super Bowl.

The 30,000 runners, the 2 million or so spectators on the streets, the volunteers and everyone else connected with the Nov. 4 event can show the world that New York is putting its best feet forward.

The five-borough marathon got started in 1976, just in time for our nation's bicentennial. New York needs this marathon more than ever before. Marathon organizers understand that the date of this race has put them and the city in a unique position. The marathon will be the city's biggest international event since Sept. 11, and that is why the New York Road Runners have to go ahead with the race. Besides, the Road Runners have heard from runners from the tri-state area, from around the country and from around the world that they want to run.

Last year's women's champion, Ludmila Petrova of Russia, is coming to defend her title. The men's champ, Morocco's Abdelkhader El Mouaziz, is not going to make it because he thinks he's not in top shape. The club has not seen a drop-off of international runners. Indeed, people seem to want to run this year to make a statement, and now the marathon is giving slots for the 2002 race because this year's roster is full.

The pre-race support is encouraging. New York needs the runners and their money. During the week leading up to the 2000 Marathon, the runners, their friends and families spent $114,693,883 in the city, according to a Road Runner spokesman. That's a huge economic impact.

This year, about a third of the runners are coming from other countries and another third from outside the tri-state region. No matter where they're coming from, you can bet they'll be using planes, trains, buses, cars, taxis, hotels, motels and restaurants.

You can also add the contributions of 12,000 volunteers. Then there's the security detail. In the past, more than 2,000 police officers have been assigned to work the race. The Road Runners maintain that security has always been a top priority, but it will indeed be heightened this year. Marathon officials are working with city, state and federal authorities to secure the 26.2 miles of streets that will be used for the race.

New York needs those people to come to the city and show that life exists only eight weeks after the horrific attacks. The Marathon has designated 21 "official" hotels and has engaged three airlines as corporate partners. The international media will also be in an ideal position to show the city for what it is: the financial, arts and cultural capital of the United States.

The point of the New York City Marathon has always been inclusion. Look at the race participants, look at the neighborhoods the runners pass through. Look at the spectators lining the streets, giving out water and offering encouragement to people they don't even know. They show the spirit of the Big Apple at its best.

The New York City Marathon is more than a major race to bring the city and its people together. It's an international athletic event. It's also a big chance for New York to show off and tell the world we may have been knocked down, but we're back on our feet and running as fast as we can.

GOP Politics Cast a Shadow Over the Super Bowl
Newsday, New York City, January 21, 2003

The Super Bowl has got me thinking a lot about politics and football. Both are blood sports, with a clear-cut winner and a loser. Look at the eerie similarity between Al Gore's 2000 presidential campaign and the 2002 New York Giants season, for example.

Gore started strong, faded in the middle but came back with a rush, and on Election Day had a chance at the end to win—only to see it taken away by the officials. The Giants started strong, faded in the middle, came back with a rush and on their decisive day had their chance at the end to win—only to see it taken away by the officials. At least in the Giants' case, unlike Gore's, they didn't lose because of "hanging chads" (as in Jets' Quarterback Chad Pennington's overthrown passes, which did in the Jets). We all know what happened to Gore's ballots in Florida. But what's done is done, and it's on to San Diego and the Super Bowl, the biggest game in the country—on the field and off.

The National Football League consists of 32 teams with owners who are highly connected to the national political scene in Washington and in their local communities.

New York Jets owner Robert Wood Johnson IV's team won't be playing on the "Pennington seed" grass field in the San Diego stadium that was once named after Mets broadcaster Bob Murphy's brother, Jack. Brooklyn's Al Davis's Raiders beat New Jersey Johnson's Jets.

But Johnson's big game is yet to be played. Johnson is a major Republican political fund-raiser in New Jersey and a top contributor to George W. Bush's 2000 presidential campaign. He wants to take his Jets and move them across the Hudson River to Manhattan's West Side—if he can get a new stadium.

Johnson would have to play ball with New York's Republican Gov. George Pataki and a Democrat-turned-Republican Mayor Michael Bloomberg to get funding for the venture.

Besides knowing how and where to find money, Johnson also has one additional weapon in his arsenal, the promise of a 2013 Super Bowl, which was revealed by the NFL last October. Johnson can use the Super Bowl as a carrot in persuading Pataki, Bloomberg and other good New York Republicans that an Olympic/Jets Stadium might be a good idea in Manhattan.

Do you think Pataki isn't paying close attention to Johnson's needs, despite the Empire State's budget woes? Even if the governor isn't listening, Bloomberg has been pushing for two Super Bowls since last fall (2008 for the Giants being the first one) and he'll have a contingent lobbying in San Diego. Bloomberg is 100 percent behind Commissioner Paul Tagliabue's proposal to bring the 2008 event to Giants Stadium and the 2013 game to a new West Side stadium. It isn't often that the mayor of New York City would push for East Rutherford to land a competitive business, but Bloomberg knows that most of the Super Bowl tie-in activities would take place east of the Hudson. Whether he can score the Big Game will be learned sometime this fall.

Johnson isn't the only Republican who has enormous political clout within the National Football League. In fact, if you ask Brooklyn native and present Baltimore Ravens owner Art Modell about his NFL peers, he will tell you that it's a group made up of 32 Republicans who believe in socialism when it comes to professional football. Modell was once so popular in Ohio, when he owned the Cleveland Browns, that the Republicans wanted him to run for mayor in Cleveland or even challenge Democrat John Glenn for a Senate seat. He did neither and left Cleveland in the lurch for a better stadium deal in Maryland.

This Sunday's Big Game is where Alex Spanos' San Diego Chargers play from August through December. Spanos is a 78-year-old self-made millionaire who was among the major contributors to the Bush 2000 campaign. He has a well-known antipathy toward the Raiders, whom he has to host this weekend. Spanos has long been unhappy with his stadium deal, as he once told me, and would like to get a new football arena in San Diego as soon as possible. For Spanos, that could be after the 2003 season, but Spanos really doesn't have too many options.

Now you would think that Spanos is so pro-Bush that he would detest the thought of ever enlisting someone who worked with President Bill Clinton in the White House to help him land a new venue. Wrong!

Alex Spanos hired Mark Fabiani, a former White House aide under Clinton, and chief of staff of ex-Los Angeles Mayor Tom Bradley, to get him a new stadium in San Diego. Bringing Fabiani in for someone like Spanos must have been like the New York Giants hiring Leo Durocher after the Brooklyn Dodgers fired him in 1948. It must have seemed unappealing in some ways, but in blood sports you play to win.

Big Game, Big Business

The Baltimore Sun, January 26, 2003

America is a nation of local sports fans, as Orioles and Ravens backers can tell you. But there is only one sports event that captivates and has an impact on every community in the nation from Maine to this year's host, San Diego, and all points in-between.

The Super Bowl.

The Super Bowl is uniquely American. The Fourth of July is America's birthday party, but the Super Bowl is America's excuse for a party. Supermarkets have "super sales" for countless "super" parties. Super Bowl Sunday is the second-biggest day of food consumption behind only Thanksgiving. The Super Bowl is the top at-home party event of the year, surpassing New Year's Eve.

According to the National Electronic Dealers Association, sales of large screen TVs increase 500 percent during Super Bowl week because the event increases demand for television sets to watch the "big game."

The Beer Institute has data that suggests the Super Bowl is one of the seven biggest sales days of the year behind only Thanksgiving, Christmas, New Year's Eve and the Fourth of July.

Newspapers sell advertising for special Super Bowl sections. The Super Bowl is a moneymaker for supermarkets, department stores, bars, snack food makers, breweries and restaurants.

It also is the springboard for companies to start their annual TV, radio and print advertising campaigns.

But it wasn't always like this.

In 1967, it was just the World Championship Game, AFL vs. NFL. The game was held in the 94,000-seat Los Angeles Memorial Coliseum with tickets available for $12, $10 and $6, and roughly 33,000 seats went unsold. It was the last time a Super Bowl or the World Championship Game was not a sellout. Both CBS and NBC televised the game, each using the same TV feed with different announcers and different advertisers.

Today, thanks in great part to Joe Namath and the New York Jets beating the heavily favored Baltimore Colts on Jan. 12, 1969, in the first "named" Super Bowl, it's no longer NFL vs. AFL, NFL advertisers vs. AFL advertisers, CBS vs. NBC. In fact, the Disney-owned ABC-TV network broadcasts the game every three years along with Fox and CBS. But in 1967, the American Football League and the Kansas City Chiefs were considered by Vince Lombardi, the Green Bay Packers and the NFL to be part of a "Mickey Mouse league."

The name "Super Bowl," with its Roman numerals, wasn't a product of any focus group or brainstorming sessions. Kansas City Chiefs owner Lamar Hunt, who founded the AFL because he couldn't get an NFL team in Dallas, thought up the name while he was watching his kids play with a multicolored ball.

"They each had a Super Ball that my wife had given to them and they were always talking about them, and I just used the expression Super Bowl," he said. "It was an accidental thing."

NFL Commissioner Pete Rozelle didn't like the name, nor did NFL owners. Still, the game had no name and no one had suggested anything else.

Ironically, the Super Ball was a super dud. Wham-O began producing a ball made of Zectron in 1965, two years before Super Bowl I was played. After only a few years, competitors copied Wham-O's "double-top secret" formula for Zectron, and the Super Ball was out of production by 1976.

"I don't know how much money the Super Bowl means," Mr. Hunt said, "but it's all from a child's toy ball." Even Mr. Rozelle would eventually concede that the "super" name probably played a major role in the event's success.

The event has become so successful that cities bid for the game. It brings in tens of thousands of visitors who spend about $300 million during the Super Bowl week festivities.

The Super Bowl will generate millions of dollars for the ailing airline industry, hotels and motels, rent-a-car agencies and the food industry in San Diego. Across the country, the Super Bowl means money for other businesses.

NBA Draft May Give Knicks Nothing But Air
Newsday, New York City Edition, May 20, 2003

For Spike Lee, Woody Allen and other high-rolling Knicks fans willing to pay more than $1,500 to see a basketball game in Madison Square Garden, this Thursday could be the night that the Knickerbockers' fortunes turn around, if the right ping-pong ball connected to a talented teenager pops up in an industrial park in Secaucus—not far from the Meadowlands home of the defending Eastern Conference Champions, George Steinbrenner's New Jersey Nets.

The ping-pong ball is in National Basketball Commissioner David Stern's NBA Draft Lottery. You have to be in it to win it, and the way you get in it is by being a bad basketball team during the regular season. Charles Dolan's Knicks certainly qualified on that account. Of course, New York wasn't as awful as Denver or Cleveland or Toronto or Miami. The Knicks were just mediocre, and that means that the Knicks' chances of landing one of the top three spots in June's NBA Draft are as slim as stopping Jason Kidd on a fastbreak. In a chamber of 1,000 bouncing ping-pong balls, the Knicks only have 15.

Hey, you never know.

The Nets, who have overshadowed Dolan's Knicks in the past two years, are making a championship run thanks in no small part to hitting the 2000 NBA lottery and drafting Kenyon Martin as their first pick.

This year the best three players in the 2003 NBA Draft are teenagers. The much heralded and hyped Lebron James from Akron, Ohio, is supposed to be the next great player. Then there is Darko Milicic from Serbia-Montenegro and finally Syracuse University's Carmelo Anthony, the 18-year-old who led the Orange Men to the 2003 NCAA Championship. All three would look good in a Knicks uniform. They aren't the only teenagers who want to enter the NBA. In fact, there are a good many 18- and 19-year-olds who want in, and their youth seems to be bothering David Stern, NBA owners, college presidents, athletic directors, basketball coaches and the venerable guardians of basketball, the sportswriters.

As recently as the eve of the Iraq conflict, Stern was leaning on the NBA's players association to change its view on teenagers in the workplace and agree to a 20-year-old minimum entry age.

Stern doesn't think James should be in his pro league and would like to deny him and other teenagers who just graduated high school an opportunity to earn a living playing professional basketball. Stern and his owners would like to see them play college basketball for nothing and gain experience in that setting so they could become more polished players, which would, in theory, raise the level of play in Stern's industry.

Here's a note to the commissioner: The U.S. military begins recruiting future soldiers in high school, trying to persuade 16- and 17-year-old kids to join one of its armed forces upon graduation. Some of those teenagers who signed up are now serving our country quite capably in Afghanistan or Iraq.

Commissioner Stern is a brilliant man. He knows just how young U.S. soldiers are, and that teenagers are performing dangerous duty daily. He knows that the military trusts teenagers to undertake difficult missions.

What exactly is so hazardous about a teenager joining the Cleveland Cavaliers, Memphis Grizzlies or the New York Knickerbockers? Getting fouled going down the lane? Being late for practice? Having Spike Lee yell at you in the Garden? Or maybe Jack Nicholson giving you abuse in L.A.?

Stern's argument rings hollow. Very hollow and maybe illegal as well, since he is denying employment to high school graduates over the age of 18. Both Major League Baseball and the National Hockey League draft 18-year-olds. Golf and tennis feature teenage players. There is no age limit for the music business or Hollywood. So how can Stern and the NBA impose a minimum-age requirement? That's easily accomplished in theory—all Stern needs is for the National Basketball Players Association to go along with his scheme.

And that's Stern's biggest problem. Getting the players to agree. NBPA Executive Director Billy Hunter isn't ready to implement Stern's plan. His group has been stonewalling for more than two years now.

There is another component in all this as well. It's called money. Players entering the NBA after being selected in the first round sign three-year entry contracts. Under this rule, an 18-year-old can become a free agent at the tender age of 21—as Tracy McGrady did, being drafted by Toronto and then signing with Orlando. Should Stern and the team owners get their way, players entering the league at 20 could not become free agents until they're 23. It's far easier for an owner to make an economic decision on a more proven 23-year-old than a 21-year-old. That's what the owners are really shooting for. They don't want to gamble their money on a player who may never reach his potential.

Stern is making the wrong call on age restrictions. The military, which is far more perilous and pays significantly less than a professional sport, recruits teenagers. So do many other businesses. And so should the NBA—because Chuck Dolan's Knicks need all the help they can get.

Sports Won't Tolerate Prejudice
Metro [Philly], October 9, 2003

For those who dismiss sports as just a game with sticks and balls, this may come as a major surprise. Sports matters in the American society and what sports people say is carefully monitored as Rush Limbaugh found out last week. Why is it that sports people face far greater scrutiny when they talk?

There is a pretty simple answer, and it lies in sports' basic appeal. There are so many levels to sports. It attracts the country's biggest capitalists who invest in sports franchises. The industry's clientele comes from every social group from the very, very rich to the poorest of the poor, from the very young to the very old. Sports cuts across racial barriers.

Men and women not only watch, but they were and are participants in some sports genre, whether it's a game with sticks and balls or just running on the street. Sports belong to people of all sizes, shapes and colors.

Politicians devise all sorts of spending programs, using taxpayers money, to attract major league teams, so they can make the claim that their city or state is in the big league. So when someone connected to sports says something offensive, the word gets out quickly, as Al Campanis learned in 1987, as Jimmy the Greek, Marge Schott and John Rocker found out.

Unlike Campanis, the Greek, Schott and Rocker, Rush Limbaugh wasn't prodded into saying anything offensive. Limbaugh was appearing as part of ESPN's Sunday night pre-game show that previewed the Philadelphia Eagles-Buffalo Bills game. This wasn't the April 6, 1987 edition of *Nightline with Ted Koppel* who on April 6, 1987 got Los Angeles Dodgers General Manager Al Campanis to say that blacks may not have some of the necessities to be, let's say, a field manager, or perhaps a general manager. A year later, Jimmy the Greek gave an interview on Martin Luther King Day at a Washington restaurant to a local television station. The CBS sportscaster said, "The black is a better athlete to begin with, because he has been bred to be that way. This goes all the way back to the Civil War, when the slave owner would breed his big black to his big woman so that he could have a big black kid, see."

Major League Baseball suspended Cincinnati Reds owner Marge Schott for nine months in 1992 after a former Reds employee said that Schott called two of her players Eric Davis and Dave Parker "million-dollar n———rs," and also that she owned a swastika arm band.

She put out a news release saying that she didn't mean to offend anyone by using the word "n———r" and by owning Nazi memorabilia. Four years later, Schott was suspended again after saying that Adolf Hitler "was good in the beginning, but went too far." In December 1999, Braves pitcher John Rocker gave a memorable interview to *Sports Illustrated* when he went on an anti-New York, anti-immigration tirade. Rocker was suspended and shortly thereafter his career was in tatters.

Limbaugh's diatribe on the NFL pre-game show mirrored what he has been saying for the past 15 years on his three-hour daily radio show, except this time it was different. What Limbaugh forgot is that sports in American society matters and that sports is a place where ignorance and prejudice are not tolerated and that is the best attribute that the sports world has to offer.

Politics

Vallone at Fault for Yankee Woes, by George
Street & Smith's Sports Business Journal, June 29–July 6, 1998

It's Peter Vallone's fault, by George. The principal owner of the New York Yankees now has a scapegoat if indeed he decides to pull the Yankees out of the Bronx after the 2002 baseball season and move to New Jersey.

Why is Vallone being vilified by a tenant who stiffed his landlord, New York City, in rent? Vallone, the New York City Council president, has suggested that city taxpayers should have a say in whether New York should spend billions of dollars on a new baseball park on Manhattan's West Side.

Vallone wants to put the issue before voters in November. Mayor Rudolph Giuliani doesn't, and neither does Steinbrenner. A referendum becomes a political campaign, and this could be a rough one.

Steinbrenner now says Vallone is pushing the Yankees out of New York, and the New York Yankees could become the New Jersey Yankees in 2003.

Steinbrenner cannot finger Bronx Borough President Fernando Ferrer; certainly not Giuliani; not Gov. George Pataki, who favors the Bronx site as the Yankees' home; not Sen. Alphonse D'Amato. Not the Community Boards in Manhattan. Not the environmentalists. Not even Sen. Daniel Patrick Moynihan, who would like to close the loopholes in the 1986 tax act that allow municipalities to go out and build stadiums and arenas.

See, it really is Peter Vallone's fault. No one else is to blame.

Is Steinbrenner bluffing? Probably not, because he knows getting a stadium out of New York City voters may be a difficult task. All Steinbrenner has to do is go back in history, all the way back to the first Tuesday in May 1998.

On May 5, voters in the Triad region of North Carolina, which includes Greensboro, soundly rejected a stadium referendum by a 2-to-1 ratio. Voters were asked to support a restaurant tax that would have raised about $150 million to build a stadium for a group headed by businessman Don Beaver.

Beaver had agreed to purchase the Minnesota Twins and move them to North Carolina in 1999. Actually, the relocated Twins would have played two years in a minor league park in South Carolina near Charlotte before moving to Greensboro.

One of the arguments that stadium proponents in North Carolina used was that the arena area needed a major league team to keep 18-to-24-year olds in the area. The team would give them something to do.

New York does not need the Yankees to give Generation X-ers something to do. Besides, Generation X-ers really don't like baseball all that much. Baseball is trying to reinvigorate interest in people under 35.

In Pittsburgh, voters said no to the Pirates' request for a new ballpark last November. But that hasn't stopped Pittsburgh from figuring out a way to produce a new stadium for the Bucs. Seattle voters said no to a new Mariners park, but politicians figured out how to build a new stadium. Voters also rejected a Milwaukee park, but a special tax district was set up and Miller Park is being erected.

Saying no does not mean saying no. After all, New Jersey voters rejected building a baseball stadium in 1985, and Steinbrenner seems to think he can get one anyway.

Steinbrenner probably doesn't want to get involved in a political campaign either. He had a little trouble with campaign contributions back in 1972 with the Nixon team. He did not get his pardon until the final day of Ronald Reagan's term in 1989.

Still, all in all, it's Peter Vallone's fault, by George.

'Cablevision 5' Dishing Up a Frivolous Suit
The Bergen Record, April 19, 2002

At a time when the courts are filled with frivolous lawsuits, here comes another one. Five Cablevision subscribers, who want their YES TV, are going before a U. S. District judge on April 22 in Central Islip and demanding their YES TV.

The Cablevision-Yankee hostages are asking that Cablevision carry blacked out Yankee games while negotiations between Cablevision and YES continue. They also want some money for whatever damages they are incurring by not being able to watch the Yankees on cable TV.

Here's a bit of advice for the Cablevision 5.

Your story is touching and sad to be sure. Being deprived of what you think is your right to watch baseball. But you are wasting taxpayers' dollars and the court's time with your heart-wrenching tale of woe. That is because you don't have the right to watch a baseball game, believe it or not, on cable TV, nor do you have the right to make other people pay for your entertainment which will happen if you by some fluke happen to win this case and get the Yankees YES Network as a basic channel.

Another note to the Cablevision 5. Get out of the courts and go to your local town and village governments and read the franchise agreements between those municipalities and the local cable operator. You might find that laws need to be re-written because cable operators were given monopoly powers by local lawmakers when communities were being wired.

Back in the Sixties and Seventies, those who decided to invest in the new cable TV industry pointed out that the investors were spending a lot of money wiring homes and apartments. So the cable investors asked for protection against those who might be competitors and use their cable lines. The local lawmakers agreed with the cable TV investors and thus a regulated industry was born.

The crux of the YES Network vs. Cablevision conflict is that both sides are correct, but not for the proper reasons. George Steinbrenner and the YES Network have every right to start operations and demand that their product be placed on a basic cable channel.

Cablevision Chairman Charles Dolan can entertain offers but in the end he has the right to reject those demands. Dolan's New York Knickerbockers had to make a decision on Patrick Ewing and eventually said no, shipping him out to Seattle. That's what negotiations are all about. Sports fans have no say in any of the decisions that are being made.

It is a fact that cable TV, like sports, is a monopoly. Once a cable company is granted a franchise in a local municipality, it is almost impossible to oust them. But it can be done and in 2001, Houlton, Maine, switched cable operators after the public complained of poor service.

If the Cablevision 5 plaintiffs are really interested in the integrity of cable TV, they should be redirecting their efforts and complain to New York City Mayor Michael Bloomberg and his counterparts in every town and village that has enfranchised Cablevision. Make your thoughts known to every municipality, every local mayor and every city, town or village council that has a deal with Cablevision. Start a grass roots movement with people disenchanted with their local cable system and complain to cable advisory boards. If the politicians don't listen, don't re-elect them. Use the political process.

Suing the YES Network is frivolous. YES has demanded to be on basic cable and sure many New York, New Jersey and Connecticut cable operators have reached agreements with Steinbrenner—whether their consumers want YES or not—for two reasons. The cable systems' operators felt it was either worthwhile programming, or those companies didn't want to be dragged into a fight with Steinbrenner and incur the wrath of a minority of their subscribers, Yankee fans.

And one more thing. What the Cablevision 5 and Yankee fans who are complaining loudly about not getting their YES TV have forgotten in this battle is the fairness of the Yankee agreement with cable operators. Should non-baseball fans and others who don't ever watch a baseball game or a sports event be forced to pay for the programming? The answer should be no. And those cable companies should be held accountable for raising prices without giving consumers choices.

For all of their apparent concern about the righteousness of cable television and Cablevision, the Cablevision 5 would be better served by paying attention to cable TV franchise license renewal.

NFL Lobs Jets an Easy Pass to the West Side
Newsday, New York City Edition, May 15, 2002

Excuse my skepticism, but is National Football League Commissioner Paul Tagliabue pushing for a New York area Super Bowl in February 2007 to help rebuild New York's economy after the Sept. 11 terrorist attack, as he claims, or does he have something else in mind? Such as getting New York City to help Jets owner Robert Wood Johnson IV build a $900 million stadium/arena and entertainment complex that would house the Jets as well as the Knicks, the Liberty's and the Rangers on Manhattan's West Side?

Even if Johnson and Madison Square Garden Chairman Charles Dolan pay for the actual athletic facility, the complex may cost tax-payers billions of dollars with the city and state picking up the tab for building such things as mass transit, roads and sewer lines. The city doesn't have the money for professional sports right now. Look at Mayor Michael Bloomberg's budget woes.

Is it worth spending public money for private enterprises such as the Jets and the Madison Square Garden teams? No.

Professional sports don't employ enough people or bring enough of a tax base to municipalities, as study after study has shown. Madison Square Garden doesn't pay any property taxes right now. How much would this new West Side complex bring in? You can bet it won't be enough, whatever it is.

Last fall, Tagliabue and the NFL had their chance to pump some $300 million into our region's economy by holding the 2002 Super Bowl at the Meadowlands. But after floating the idea, the league kept the game in New Orleans, as originally planned. That Super Bowl would have been more valuable to our financial recovery than one taking place five years from now.

NFL owners are meeting this week in Houston to discuss league matters, but it's unlikely that they will rule on Tagliabue's proposal until the league's October conferences in Manhattan.

So far, the 32 owners don't seem very interested in a New York Super Bowl. America's excuse for a party requires an average daily February temperature of over 50 degrees for all the pre-game festivities. Unless global warming gets here by 2007, New York doesn't have the climate that NFL owners want for their week-long football orgy.

The New Jersey Meadowlands, which will be 31 years old in 2007, would require a major renovation, but Johnson and the NFL seem to have another goal in mind. They want to get the Jets into a new stadium in time for the 2009 season (the team's Meadowlands lease runs out in 2008). The Jets' vision of a West Side stadium dovetails with the New York City 2012 Olympic Bid Committee's goal of putting an Olympic Stadium over the West Side rail yards. But both Johnson and the Olympic Committee are working against the clock. The NFL's deadline for the 2007 Super Bowl seems to be the end of October and the United States Olympic Committee is scheduled to select its candidate for the 2012 Olympics on Nov. 3.

It seems Tagliabue's ploy may have worked, though. The Super Bowl promise has reportedly captured a great deal of attention within the Bloomberg administration, but it doesn't stop with a stadium idea. Instead, the city is looking into spending some $1.5 billion to extend the No. 7 line from Seventh Avenue west and south to 34th Street as part of the area's redevelopment.

But where is that money coming from? If the city plows funds into extending the No. 7 line, what happens with the proposed Second Avenue line or the reconstruction of the area around Ground Zero or other projects in the outer boroughs? There is only so much public money available.

Pushing mass transit is a new twist on the baseball stadium idea that then-Gov. Mario Cuomo first proposed in 1993. Both Cuomo and Mayor Rudolph Giuliani fell in love with the notion of a sports complex between 11th and 12th Avenues and 32nd and 34th Streets. But it went nowhere.

Local residents in that neighborhood want no part of a stadium. Who can blame them? Can you imagine the traffic snarls and other problems associated with 80,000 people trying to get into that area on game day? The community would be paralyzed for hours.

Tagliabue may have thought he was doing New York a favor by suggesting that the NFL could hold its 2007 Super Bowl as a way to help the city's economy, but in the end, Tagliabue's offer may only help Johnson's personal economy by giving him additional leverage with Bloomberg and Gov. George Pataki in the biggest sports contest of all—the stadium game.

College Sports is Broken, Not Title IX

Bergen Record, February 6, 2003

Is the Bush Administration waging war against women's rights? That answer may come this spring after Secretary of Education Rod Paige finishes his review of Title IX legislation that bans sex discrimination in colleges, whether it is in college admissions, getting a teaching job or on the college sports playing field.

The Secretary of Education's Committee on Opportunities in Athletics has been meeting for the past year and will make its recommendations to Secretary Paige on February 28. There is some nervousness among women's groups including The Women's Sports Foundation and the Coalition for Women and Girls in Education that the Bush Administration may change some of the rules that were signed into law by President Richard Nixon in 1972.

The Bush Administration has not tipped its hand on what it might do, but given the President's views on abortion and that the White House has joined in as a friend of the court in the University of Michigan affirmative action case that will be heard by the Supreme Court, there is some justification for the anxiety.

The White House filed a brief with the court claiming that the University of Michigan's admissions policies, which award students a significant number of extra points based solely on their race and establish numerical targets for incoming minority students, are unconstitutional.

The Title IX law didn't establish numerical targets for minorities; instead it guaranteed rights. The law states: "No person in the U.S. shall, on the basis of sex be excluded from participation in, or denied the benefits of, or be subjected to discrimination under any educational program or activity receiving federal aid."

Title IX has changed how college sports are played in the country. Prior to 1972, U.S. General Accounting Office released a figure showing that 32,000 women had participated in college sports and that figure grew to 163,000 by 1999.

Men no longer get 95 percent of the dollars earmarked for sports and that is causing friction in the men's teams coaching fraternity. A good number of those coaches think Title IX has taken away their ability to get the best athletes for their teams because they can't spend scholarship money solely for men's teams.

Men's sports programs have been eliminated at schools. But, oddly enough, Title IX was never meant to level out the college sports playing field and give women sports opportunities. Title IX's original intent was to give women a fair chance at being accepted in a school and for women professors to get equal opportunity at advancing within the system.

Title IX has worked. By 1994, women received 38 percent of medical degrees earned in the US, compared with 9 percent in 1972; 43 percent of law degrees, compared with 7 percent in 1972 and 44 percent of all doctoral degrees, up from 25 percent in 1977.

Title IX is too tied into sports. And that brings a more significant question that needs to be answered. Should colleges and universities be in the big-time sports business? College sports has become a $5 billion a year industry and schools are paying as much as $2 million a year for football coaches. Title IX opponents say that men's sports, particularly football and basketball, are funding entire school sports programs and that it is unfair for men to lose out on scholarship opportunities because men's sports generate dollars for the schools.

The Title IX argument comes down to money and who should get it for sports.

Are men more deserving of the money because they take part in traditional sporting events or are women equal partners? The answer should be that women are equals.

But the Bush Administration may change the Title IX law sometime this year because of pressure from men's team coaches wanting more money for their teams and that's wrong.

Title IX has created diversity in society and is not just a piece of sports legislation. No matter what the jocks say.

And do you know what else is wrong? Colleges and universities should not be farm systems for the National Football League and the National Basketball Association. They should be institutions of higher education first and foremost.

Big time college sports are broken, not Title IX.

Why Are Rich Teams Getting City's Millions?
Newsday, New York City Edition, June 17, 2003

It's not quite the fall classic, but for Mets fans this weekend's Subway Series could be the highlight of a season that has gone south. The Mets are in the cellar, yet their fans can claim some bragging rights if somehow the Amazin's can win two of the three games at home against the Yankees.

Truth be told, this hasn't been the kind of year that Yankees fans can be too smug about, either. Judged by previous years' standards, the Yankees have been arguably mediocre.

And that brings up the question: Is the city of New York, which is giving both the Mets and Yankees $5 million each for stadium research and development, getting its money's worth from Fred Wilpon's Mets or George Steinbrenner's Yankees—the teams with the top two payrolls in the major leagues?

The answer is no.

Believe it or not, with the city going through a major budget crisis that has seen the closing of firehouses, the slashing of social services to the poor and the elderly, and the hiking of bus and subway fares, train tickets and car tolls along with property and sales taxes, the city continues to give both Wilpon and Steinbrenner millions of dollars each for R and D. Where it actually goes is anybody's guess.

It's part of a deal struck by Mayor Rudolph Giuliani, an ardent Yankees fan, which gave the two teams $50 million over a five-year period to study what type of stadiums should be built to replace Shea and Yankee Stadium. It was kind of an odd deal because, since the late 1990s, Wilpon has had plans on the table to build Ebbets Field II in Shea's left-field parking area, and, if it is ever built, Steinbrenner would be getting his new structure just yards away from the famed Bronx ballpark.

But it's unfair to single out Wilpon and Steinbrenner for taking advantage of the Big Apple's largesse. After all, the city does have two other big-league teams, the Knicks and the Rangers that play on some prime real estate taking up two city blocks from 31st to 33rd Street between 7th and 8th Avenues.

Cablevision Chairman Charles Dolan, who owns Madison Square Garden, doesn't pay any property taxes. But don't blame Dolan for this one. The Garden's previous owners, Gulf and Western, convinced politicians back in the 1980s that it would move the Knicks to Long Island and the Rangers to New Jersey because doing business in Manhattan was too expensive and that neither the Knicks nor the Rangers would be able to compete with other NHL and NBA teams if their owner had to pay onerous property taxes and utilities.

Politicians here and in Albany caved in. But have city and state residents gotten their money's worth from the Rangers, who won a Stanley Cup in 1994 but have missed the playoffs for six straight years, and the Knicks, who haven't won a title since 1973 and have also missed the playoffs the past two years?

The answer is of course not.

The fans may not know it, but sports teams have long been on the government dole. Cleveland was the first city to use taxpayers' dollars to build a stadium, in part to attract the 1932 Summer Olympics. (Does that story have a familiar ring here in New York?) Cleveland spent $2.5 million for a 78,000-seat stadium, but Los Angeles got the Olympics and spent $950,000 to upgrade the existing Los Angeles Coliseum.

Milwaukee was the first city to actively seek a Major League Baseball team by putting up $5 million to build a stadium. By 1953, the stadium was complete and Milwaukee cobbled together a financial deal to move the Boston Braves to the Midwest. Milwaukee led the league in attendance and Brooklyn Dodgers owner Walter O'Malley, still playing in decaying Ebbets Field, took notice. O'Malley wanted a taxpayer-funded new park in Brooklyn but met stiff resistance from Robert Moses, who felt that O'Malley could afford to build his own stadium.

Eventually Moses suggested Flushing Meadows as an alternative for both O'Malley and New York Giants owner Horace Stoneham, who was also looking for greener pastures for his baseball team. O'Malley went to Los Angeles; Stoneham to San Francisco. Moses' Flushing Meadows ballpark did become a reality in 1964 when Shea Stadium opened. Shea was a relative bargain, costing New Yorkers an estimated $28.5 million dollars, and it's still operational 39 years later, about the best thing you can say for it.

Moses' park will come alive this weekend as the Mets host the Yankees. While fans in attendance pay for overpriced beer and pretzels and watch the woeful Mets and the contending Yankees, they should ponder this question: Are we getting our money's worth out of our four New York big league teams?

The answer is no.

Cities Prefer Sports Parks to Power
Metro [Philly], September 3, 2003

The numbers coming from the Bush Administration are staggering. It's going to cost at least $50 billion to upgrade the country's aging electrical power grid. The Philadelphia area was lucky back on August 14 and 15. People had electricity but it could have been far different. Regardless, Philadelphia residents will eventually have to pay more for power.

And when you start thinking about the cost to bring the nation's power grid up to 21st century state-of-the-art technology, the final price may actually be less than the money taxpayers have put into baseball parks, football stadiums and indoor arenas across the country.

After all, Philadelphia is paying more than a billion dollars for the Eagles' and Phillies' new workstations (taxpayers are picking up one-third of the bill). And that's without taking into account paying off interest on the debt. So maybe rebuilding the power infrastructure is a bargain compared to what we have paid for new and renovated sports facilities nationally.

The Oregon State Legislature recently passed a bill that could allocate hundreds of millions of dollars as seed money for the construction of a Major League Baseball park in Portland. Those politicians should have studied what happened in Cleveland during the Northeast blackout before they decide to dole out hundreds of millions of dollars.

Cleveland, which has spent probably a billion dollars on sports facilities, apparently doesn't have back up power generators to keep its water supply going when there is an energy disruption. But it did have money for the cosmetic and elitist entertainment that major league sports has evolved into.

Baseball Commissioner Fay Vincent in the early 1990s threatened Cleveland officials, telling them that the city would lose its baseball team if the city didn't come forward with money to build a new baseball park. City officials cobbled together a proposal to raise the tax on tobacco and alcohol sold in Cleveland to pay for the stadium. Voters agreed in a referendum vote that the Indians should have a new facility and the Indians were saved. At roughly the same time, the city put up money for a new indoor arena for the NBA's Cleveland Cavaliers to go along with the stadium and the Rock and Roll Hall of Fame.

In 1995, Browns owner Art Modell concluded that the city had no money for his NFL team and moved to Baltimore. By 1998, the NFL returned to Cleveland and opened a taxpayer funded new football facility.

After the blackout, some 1.5 million Cleveland area residents were told to boil their water because no one was sure if the tap water was clean enough to drink. Detroit and Michigan have spent $320 million for new facilities for the Tigers and Lions, but had water problems from the power outage. Having a major league team is worthless if people can't get to games because governments didn't invest in infrastructure like power grids.

Philadelphia was lucky on Aug.14 and 15. But here's a question that needs to be asked. Did the city give thought to emergencies when it allocated millions upon millions of dollars to build new sports facilities?

You might not want to know the answer.

New Jersey's Loss Could Be Brooklyn's Gain
Newsday, New York City Edition, September 16, 2003

I took a ride over the Manhattan Bridge a few Saturday nights ago and stopped at Atlantic Avenue just to look at a hole in the ground that has some rail lines running through it. This isn't just any hole, mind you. Robert Moses thought that this hole could have been the new home of the Brooklyn Dodgers but Walter O'Malley wasn't impressed with it and took his team to LA.

This cavity in Brooklyn continues to tantalize potential developers. The latest are Lewis Katz and Bruce Ratner. Katz is one of the owners of the New Jersey Nets and Devils. Ratner is a real estate guy who may want to buy into the teams. Both look at that hole and envision an arena along with office space and a huge housing complex—some 5,500 apartments according to some reports. The arena would house the NBA's Brooklyn Nets and NHL's Brooklyn Devils. Well, maybe they would have to change the name because the legendary Jersey Devil isn't likely to leave the New Jersey pinelands.

But coming up with names for relocated franchises is the least of their problems. Although downtown Brooklyn might be a good spot in terms of mass transit to build an arena, there are many hoops to go through before it becomes reality.

Just what is the present Nets ownership thinking? You wonder whether Katz and his major money man Ray Chambers are talking to George Steinbrenner, one of their other Nets partners, about the economic problems of playing in a building at the Meadowlands that is 22 years old—ancient by stadium standards. Or are the Nets owners and Steinbrenner planning a divorce, since the Yankee-Nets marriage is apparently on the rocks?

Another factor behind this is the future of the proposed Newark Arena, which would house the Nets and Devils. Does New Jersey have the money to spend on a Newark sports center? According to Gov. James McGreevy, the answer is no. So, if the Nets-Devils owners want the state to renovate the Meadowlands, they better be prepared to kick in some money of their own to get the Meadowlands up to 2003 standards. That means installing more luxury boxes, upgrading premium seats, and kicking out less wealthy Nets and Devils patrons, in other words, their average fans.

Because spending their own money on an old sports facility seems to go against the grain of today's big- league team owners, that could leave Brooklyn in the lead to get the Nets. But there's another wrinkle. New York Islanders owner Charles Wang (the founder of Computer Associates) has an interest in the Nets and could move the team back to its second home—or third or fourth home, depending on who's counting—the Nassau Coliseum. The Nets started out in 1967 in the American Basketball Association as the New Jersey Americans in the Teaneck Armory and "moved" in 1968 to the Commack Arena after the armory booked another activity that conflicted with the Americans' playoff game. That forced the Americans to flee to Long Island. But when the team landed in Commack, it found out that its basketball court had been laid over the ice rink without insulation. The ice had started to melt, water had seeped through the floor, and the court was unusable. The game was cancelled. Still, the owners decided Commack was going to be their new home. Then they found the Island Garden. In 1972 the team moved to the Nassau Coliseum, becoming the NBA New York Nets, along the way. Five years later the team was sold and relocated to New Jersey.

Wang must also have real estate on his mind. His Islanders play in an even older building than the Meadowlands Arena. Wang wants a new facility, and Nassau County would like to see someone develop a hub, presumably starting in the Nassau Coliseum parking lot. But Nassau County is financially strapped, so who would pay for a new arena?

Of course, filling that Atlantic Avenue hole with a new sports facility is far more complicated than just moving two professional teams from New Jersey. Even though Mayor Michael Bloomberg has endorsed the idea, the Nets and Devils owners seem to be at the back of the line when it comes to the public trough. And dining on the taxpayers' credit card is what owning a sports franchise is all about.

Didn't Mayor Rudolph Giuliani promise Steinbrenner and Mets owner Fred Wilpon new stadiums? And isn't the city giving both teams $5 million apiece annually for stadium research and development through 2006?

You have to remember that New York is bidding for the 2012 Summer Olympics. So far, Brooklyn hasn't played a prominent role in that scheme. Jets owner Woody Johnson supposedly wants to flee the Meadowlands for Manhattan's West Side, assuming that he'd get a new sports facility as part of the Olympics development deal. And let's not forget Charles and James Dolan's Madison Square Garden, which was antiquated when it opened in 1968. Giuliani wanted to replace the present Garden as part of his grand sports vision.

But that was when New York City may have had some big bucks. With Bloomberg raising taxes, cutting back services and laying off workers, where is the money for a Brooklyn project? And filling that hole on Atlantic Avenue won't be cheap because the MTA isn't just going to hand over the air rights without some kind of return, considering that straphangers would be paying close attention.

Brooklyn is definitely in the race for the Nets and the Devils. No one knows if Katz and Ratner have a strong enough lineup to overcome both New Jersey and Nassau County. Without the juice, the Brooklyn bid will probably come up short, reviving that old Dodgers fan lament: "Wait till next year."

Budget Woes Could Foul Out High School Sports
Newsday, New York City Edition, December 2, 2003

Basketball, not baseball or football, is the city's game. Our high schools have turned out such greats as Lew Alcindor (later known as Kareem Abdul-Jabbar), Connie Hawkins, Tiny Archibald, Dick and Al Maguire and many other top players. Another high school basketball season has just begun, and who knows how many future stars are out there perfecting their jump shots for posterity? But, given what's happening around the country, how much longer will New York be able to afford to keep basketball along with some 30 other varsity sports without charging user fees?

That's a hot question because many school districts around the country—in Illinois, Massachusetts and Ohio, to name a few—are imposing fees on athletes, and the fees aren't cheap, ranging from $40 to a $1,000 per sport. The expenses add up for parents whose children play a number of sports or for parents with more than one child in school. Of course, it's a question of priorities. Last summer, school boards in Salem, Ore., were imposing user fees on school sports while the Oregon legislature was discussing ways to raise $150 million from state taxpayers to help subsidize a proposed Major League Baseball park in Portland.

You don't have to look too far to see this disturbing trend. In mid-November, the Yonkers school board laid off 502 workers and cut out virtually every after-school program, athletics included. A few days later, following a furor over the cuts, the jobs and the programs were restored, but there is no guarantee that Yonkers can keep its programs going through the end of the school year. Surviving the state's budget woes could be a close call.

So far, the city's public high school athletes haven't had to pay to play. Marty Oestreicher, the chief executive for school support services, says the city's schools athletic programs are in good shape because the athletic and physical education budget "hasn't grown or shrunk." He explains that the Bloomberg administration is "committed to education, and that physical education and athletics are part of education."

Most of the approximately $15 million the city puts into the Public Schools Athletic League goes to pay high school coaches, athletic directors, support staff at games and sports venues. A small allowance goes into equipment and uniforms. Still, according to Oestreicher, some city schools have to be creative to make ends meet. Some schools have fundraisers to pay for a bus for a road game or to get new uniforms, for example. But bake sales can only go so far. One sign of the times is a new five-year partnership with Snapple, announced last week. The $166-million plan is an exclusive vending and marketing deal between the beverage maker and the Department of Education. Certainly, without corporate sponsorship, how the city could hold its athletic budget steady is going to be a toss-up.

Around the country school funds are running dry as districts scrape bottom to keep all of their programs going.

The money has dried up, in part because of President George W. Bush's federal tax cuts, which means less money flows to states, and that in turn means less money is available to school districts. Other factors include a drop in interest rates, so school districts are getting far less on their investments, and increases in insurance coverage and security costs.

What happened to all the promises from the administration that education was a top priority?

Without a doubt children are being left behind. And that raises another issue, about equal opportunity. Everyone knows that athletics, particularly basketball, can be the ticket out of the neighborhood for many city kids. What will happen if they can't afford to play? Will high schools reward their better athletes with a grant to cover the user fees or will they treat equally all students who can't afford the fee?

That decision could change how schools get players—let alone win championships—and affect the next generation of professional athletes. Meanwhile, teaching could take a back seat to fielding a winning team, just as it does apparently at the Division-I college level. If the economy continues to sputter, high school athletes will learn a valuable civics lesson. Unfortunately, it will be at their own expense.

PA. Could Pay for More Stadiums
Metro [Philly], December 2, 2003

I recently pulled into the Holiday Inn off of Route 28 in Pittsburgh and asked the question that has become commonplace for me. "How much of the 14 percent room tax is going to the stadiums?" The clerk behind the counter pleasantly responded, "I really don't know but the Pennsylvania sales tax is six percent and the local hotel tax is five percent. When I started it was nine percent. They said they needed it for the stadiums and the Pirates started out well but then they got rid of their players and I lost interest."

Both Pennsylvanians and non-Pennsylvanians are paying a variety of taxes for a private industry, or two private industries in Pittsburgh, the baseball Pirates and the NFL's Steelers. Pennsylvanian's maybe paying for another Pittsburgh team shortly, the NHL's Penguins, who, according to team owner Mario Lemieux, need a new arena to survive. Some of the seed money for the Penguins new place will come from the old reliable source, state legislators who have passed on stadium and arena costs from sports facilities in Philadelphia, Wilkes-Barre, Scranton, Harrisburg, Hershey, Pittsburgh and other areas around the state onto taxpayers in a variety of ways from hotel/motel, car rental, sales, restaurant and water taxes to name a few.

The struggling, Midwest-based, Frontier League is interested in putting a team in Westmoreland County near Pittsburgh, and contacted state Sen. Allen Kukovich's office to see if Harrisburg had any available money to build a stadium. A Frontier League franchise needs about a 4,000- seat facility and those cost at least $6 million to build. But that's the way sports franchises operate. If a franchise owner cannot get the government to provide a facility and get a lion's share of the revenues generated by the facility flowing into the team, there will be no team. Lemieux's new arena may come to pass if the Harrisburg legislators and Gov. Rendell come up with a gaming law that allows horse racetracks to install slot machines which could lower property taxes statewide. Rendell thinks he will have the legislation on his desk and signed by Christmas.

The slot machine legislation is an essential part of Lemieux's and the Penguins' plan. If slots are placed in the tracks, then a West

Virginia racetrack owner Ted Arneault plans to go ahead and try to win support to build a racetrack near Route 28 and the Pennsylvania Turnpike Exit 48, 15 minutes from downtown Pittsburgh. If Arneault gets the track, he plans to give Lemieux some $60 million from slots revenue as part of the $275 million project. Rendell would release some $90 million in state money, the Penguins would kick in another $47 million, there would be $11.6 million coming in from federal sources, another $3 million from the Pennsylvania Water and Sewer Authority and $53 million from the Regional Asset District.

By the way, the voters have no say in stadium and/or arena decisions. In Philadelphia deals were worked out between team owners and city and state lawmakers. In Pittsburgh, voters said no to the Pirates and Steelers new stadium proposals only to see Pittsburgh, Allegheny and Harrisburg lawmakers overturn their decision. Lawmakers never say no to sports team owners because pro sports is more important than funding education or snow removal.

Terror Fear Affects Athens Olympics
Metro [Philly], April 29, 2004

Former National Football League player Pat Tillman's death in Afghanistan put a sports face onto the war on terrorism. But if you think sports and the war on terrorism are worlds apart, think again.

The sports world from Philadelphia to Lisbon, Portugal and from Athens, Greece and Athens, Ga., for that matter, has been intertwined with both military and non-military support since the September 11 attacks.

When NATO began in 1949 as a 12-nation cooperative to defend one another, it was never set up to provide protection for sports events. But NATO will be called upon to patrol the skies of Portugal to secure the UEFA Euro 2004 football (soccer) matches in June.

Portugal, which shares a long boarder with Spain, is on heightened security after the March train bombings in Madrid. Portugal will reinstate border checks, which will include examining passports and conducting vehicle inspections, and has stepped up security at transportation hubs and important public buildings.

But apparently that isn't enough to protect Euro 2004, which will feature squads from the host country Spain, Italy and the United Kingdom, all American allies in the Iraq War. Portugal wants NATO to give them assistance by using AWACS jets to provide surveillance over the country's air space and to watch out for terrorism in the skies.

This isn't the first time NATO has been asked to assist with a sporting event. In February 2002, NATO aircraft patrolled the skies around Utah during the Winter Olympics and NATO will provide aerial surveillance and sea patrols during this summer's Olympic Games.

Greece's Olympic Committee will allocate more than $1.2 billion for security and have some 45,000 people on guard including some 7,000 troops but that doesn't mean the Games will be totally secure.

An article in a London newspaper claimed the U. S. Ambassador to Greece Tom Miller told the Greek government that the United States would be pull out of the Athens Games if security in Greece was not improved. The State Department knocked down the story that first appeared in March. The United States Olympic Committee has said it has not thought of pulling out. There will, however, be an exit strategy in the event of a major terrorist attack in Greece during the Games.

It seems inconceivable that the tough talking Bush Administration would suggest that the American team would boycott the Games, but there is an increasing nervousness about Greece's ability to make the Games secure. In fact, the International Olympic Committee has taken out an insurance policy to cover themselves should the Games be interrupted or cancelled by a terrorist attack.

An Israeli-security advisor to the Games, Major General David Tsur, is worried that Greece is not up to speed with response teams should terrorists use biological or chemical weapons during the 17-day international event.

The world has changed. At one time, the biggest problem from Philadelphia to Europe was rowdy fans. Now countries like Portugal and Greece, following the United States 2002 Olympic protection lead, are requesting military assistance because of terrorist's threats. They realize that the sports and the real world are intertwined.

'Gipper' Delivered Ball for Pro Sports

The Orlando Sentinel, June 9, 2004

Ronald Reagan may have played a football hero on the screen, but in real life his tax policies made him a hero to professional sports teams that were able to expand and profit because of them.

Reagan left an enormous impact on sports by putting his signature on the Tax Reform Act of 1986.

To many sports fans, Ronald Reagan was known for two things. He was a sports announcer who "recreated" Chicago Cubs baseball games for the Des Moines, Iowa, radio station WHO, and he played the role of the dying George Gipp in a movie.

But in terms of sports, it was "Dutch" Reagan who changed league dynamics and accelerated the movement to build new stadiums and arenas complete with huge sources of potential income from luxury boxes and club seating.

It was Reagan who put the mechanism in place in 1986 that really started ownership free agency and a battle between cities for National Football League, Major League Baseball, National Basketball Association and National Hockey League teams.

The Tax Reform Act of 1986 opened a loophole in the tax laws and gave owners ammunition in their battles with cities and states to get stadiums.

The law gave municipalities a federal tax exemption on bonds to build new stadiums. The results are stunning. In 2004, 26 of the NFL's 32 teams have new stadiums or renovated facilities with enhanced revenue streams.

Of the six that have not gotten new stadiums, the New York Giants will soon partner with New Jersey to renovate Giants Stadium, and the New York Jets have plans in the works with New York City and New York state to build a new Manhattan stadium. New Orleans is getting handouts from Louisiana.

Minnesota is actively seeking a new stadium, as is Jerry Jones for the Dallas Cowboys. Wayne Huizenga operates the football stadium in Miami, which was paid for by private funding and finished in

1987 before the 1986 tax reforms kicked in for then-Miami Dolphins owner Joe Robbie and his family.

Sports-team owners started putting pressure on municipalities shortly after Congress sent the completed bill to Reagan for his approval. The frenzy then started as the Chicago White Sox ownership threatened to move to a publicly funded stadium in St. Petersburg, had the Illinois General Assembly not given approval for building a new ballpark on Chicago's South Side.

Baseball expanded to taxpayer-funded stadiums in Denver, St. Petersburg and Phoenix. Most cities built new ballparks for their Major League teams. The Yankees, Cubs, Red Sox, Dodgers, Royals, Twins, A's and Mets still play in old facilities. Baseball is looking for a taxpayer-funded stadium for the Expos.

Spring training is different, too, with little cities being forced to build state-of-the-art complexes in a bid to keep teams from leaving for better offers in other areas of Florida or Arizona.

In 1990, Major League Baseball and Minor League Baseball signed a new agreement that mandated cities and states across the country to either build new facilities or renovate existing parks by 1994, or Major League owners could pull out of those cities. It's no coincidence that independent baseball minor leagues sprung up, using cities that Major League Baseball deserted as the basis for their business ventures.

The National Hockey League was able to expand from 21 to 30 teams and relocate two Canadian-based franchises to the United States during the 1990s because of the 1986 Tax Act. The only non-U.S. city the league added was in Ottawa. Quebec City moved to Denver, Winnipeg ended up in Phoenix and the league added teams in new facilities in San Jose, Tampa, Miami, Anaheim, Nashville, Atlanta, St. Paul and Columbus, and Hartford relocated to Raleigh, N.C., when Connecticut said no to a new arena. Almost every NHL franchise has a new building with the exception of the three New York area teams and Pittsburgh.

The NBA expanded in 1987 to Orlando, Miami, Minneapolis and Charlotte. Minneapolis eventually had financial difficulty and nearly moved to New Orleans in 1994. The Minnesota legislature bailed out the team. The NBA awarded teams to Toronto and Vancouver;

the Vancouver team moved to Memphis, Charlotte ended up in
New Orleans; and Charlotte is building a taxpayer-funded arena
for its new team. Only the New York area teams have old buildings,
although the Magic ownership is unhappy with its 15-year-old
facility.

Without Ronald Reagan, the 40th president, sports in 2004 would
be a lot different. His signature on the 1986 Tax Reform Act changed
the world of sports.

Sporting Politics, Bush, Kerry in Play

The Orlando Sentinel, July 6, 2004

If virtually all of the presidential-tracking polls are correct, Republican President George W. Bush and Democratic challenger John Kerry are not only even in Florida but nationally as well. That means both campaigns are being forced to go after voters they normally would not pursue, and one of those groups is sports fans. In fact, the Bush campaign is heavily courting 18-to-34-year-old males by spending a lot of advertising dollars on ESPN in an effort to attract them.

ESPN, despite its rather low ratings, is the best known of the sports networks and has a loyal following. ESPN and the sports industry have the demographics that politicians like: young, white males who are not necessarily politically attuned but are impressionable.

And going after those potential voters is part of a strategy employed by both sides. Massachusetts Sen. Kerry has made references to the Super Bowl Champion New England Patriots, who play their games in suburban Boston, in some of his campaign speeches. Kerry has also been seen playing hockey and skiing. The winter sports may not play well in the "red" states, but Kerry does shore up his "blue" states' base. Bush hosted a NASCAR event in the White House back in December, which is popular in the "red" states, and he threw out the first pitch on Opening Day in St. Louis, in a state that he barely won back in 2000.

There is a method to the madness though. "We are trying to appeal to lots of folks," said Ken Mehlman, the campaign manager for Bush-Cheney 2004. "Our decisions about where to advertise are based on strategies. Based on looking at who watches those shows and who watches those networks and making the smart decision accordingly."

The Bush campaign is spending money on 18-to-34-year-old sports fans because it feels it can capture that demographic. But Mehlman does concede that his campaign is going after "white men largely, not exclusively, and sometimes their wives."

Although people like Mehlman say they want to appeal to all, they have targeted a very specific audience.

So it's no coincidence that Bush strategists started playing up the "NASCAR dads" theme after NASCAR champion Matt Kenseth and a large group of current and former drivers were honored last December at the White House by Bush.

Bush continued to court NASCAR dads by appearing at the Daytona 500 in February. While Bush was glad-handing racers and fans, the Republican National Committee set up shop to register potential voters.

People like Mehlman see the NASCAR fan, who is typically a Southern, white, working-class man, as a key to winning re-election. In 2000, candidate Bush won all the states that have the strongest concentration of NASCAR dads. In September 1992, the Democratic nominee Bill Clinton was booed at a NASCAR event.

The NASCAR dads might be a huge prize if people believe the growing popularity of the sport. NASCAR thinks as many as 75 million people follow its races, and the TV ratings are better than other sports like baseball, basketball and hockey during weekend blocks on Fox and NBC. Crowds of more than 100,000 at races are the norm.

Kerry and his Democratic strategists are unlikely to make much of an effort to go after the NASCAR crowd, which is why Kerry has talked about the New England Patriots, been seen trying to play pick-up hockey and vacationed at a ski slope. He is going after the same 18-to-34-year-old white voters, yet he is more likely to spend his capital on the MTV crowd. The NASCAR fan is very Republican, very patriotic, very loyal. It's a group that should be in Bush's corner.

The NASCAR dad appears to have replaced the soccer mom as the most sought-after voter of the 2004 presidential campaign and that leaves this question: Whatever happened to the soccer moms of 1996? Has motherhood changed so much that today's mothers have no stake in the 2004 election?

It would seem that Bush and Kerry should be trying to appeal to all voters' needs instead of a selected group.

And here is one other question as people try to woo the NASCAR dad and the 18-to-34-year-old male sports fans: Just how many of those people plan to vote?

Cable Decisions Could Hurt Teams' Revenue

Metro, July 19, 2004

You can't blame Yankees boss George Steinbrenner, Mets owner Fred Wilpon or Cablevision's Charles Dolan if they think the world of Fred Upton.

Upton, R-Mich., is a congressman and is the chairman of the House Subcommittee on Telecommunications and the Internet and wants to maintain the status quo when it comes to how subscribers pay for their cable television.

Currently, cable subscribers pay for every cable channel that is placed on basic expanded cable. That means most subscribers pay for ESPN, various sports channels, Lifetime, and the news networks whether they want to or not. Those channels include the highly expensive YES Network and the MSG/FOX combo, two entities that get money from 100 percent of the expanded basic cable subscribers in the tri-state area but are watched by less than five percent of those subscribers.

Neither Steinbrenner nor Dolan really wants to find out just how many people really want to pay for their channels so status quo is fine for them and their fellow owners.

But due to increasing political pressure, Upton's committee is looking into whether or not cable companies should offer their subscribers a la carte programming and give them a chance to pick and choose channels.

Upton is clearly on the side of cable's multiple systems operators and said last Wednesday that "the current business model upon which video programming and distribution relies has evolved over many years and has brought enormous benefits to the consumer."

Upton's committee is not the only Capital Hill entity looking into cable TV. The Federal Communication's Commission will hand in its report on cable TV pricing to the House Energy and Commerce Committee on Nov. 18 and FCC Commissioner Michael Copps may be ready to give cable subscribers a choice.

"It obviously sounds attractive. It gives consumers options. That's always something we ought to be looking at," Copps said recently.

"Obviously, consumers don't like to pay for something they don't watch or don't really want."

Sports owners need cable TV money to keep their franchise values high and to pay their players huge salaries. Giving people a choice instead of forcing them to take sports channels may bankrupt the sports industry, which is why the owners are counting on Upton and his colleagues to keep the status quo.

Bush & Co. Need to Get Off MLB's Back
MSNBC.com, December 9, 2004

You would think with Iraq still a mess, with the possibility of both Iran and North Korea having nuclear weapons, and the U.S. dollar continuing to fall, that both President George W. Bush and Senator John McCain would have better things to do than worry about steroid use in Major League Baseball.

But for some reason, the President and the Arizona Senator are trying to put the squeeze on the Major League Baseball Players Association to accept a stronger steroid-testing program than what is presently in effect.

Politicians like Bush and McCain keep forgetting that steroid possession without a doctor's prescription is illegal, and that has been the law of the land since 1988. If Bush or McCain really wanted to crack down on steroid use, they should start with those on the high school level and at gyms across the country. They should arrest athletes if they are caught with steroids, human growth hormones and other performance-enhancing drugs.

But there may be a business angle to all of this. In 2004, baseball had huge attendance and did big business with its corporate partners. Baseball wants to continue its so-called resurgence and may be afraid that the steroid scandal could affect the bottom line according to MLB's COO Bob Dupuy.

"We continue to assess the ramification that these issues will have on our business. It's another reason why we need to restore the confidence of not only our fans, but our partners."

Are Commissioner Bud Selig and Dupuy really concerned about the fans' trust or are they worried that their business partners like FOX, Disney, or all of those companies whose names are on ballparks might be skittish being associated with a scandal-ridden sport? Do the owners really care about the players or are they seeking to bury the scandal to save their businesses from an economic slump?

It's easy to be cynical about Selig's intent. After all, there have been people like Jose Canseco and the late Ken Caminiti who have said there was steroid usage among the players in the 1990s, but Selig and the owners turned a blind eye to the stories until recently. Until players started testifying at the San Francisco Grand Jury inquiry. Players like Barry Bonds, Jason Giambi and Gary Sheffield.

Cal Ripken's consecutive game streak and the McGwire/Sosa home run barrage that resulted in the breaking of Roger Maris's home run record are credited with helping baseball's resurgence after the 1994–95 strike. At least in the ballpark. TV ratings continue to drop and baseball acknowledges that it has to win back young fans, along with African-Americas who don't have the affinity for the sport that people over 40 years of age do.

How can the President and Congress mandate steroid testing for a private industry, an industry whose workers do not endanger the general public welfare in their workplace, the baseball diamond? Also, when did the President and Congress gain the authority to rewrite the Major League Baseball Collective Bargaining Agreement? And if Congress mandates steroid testing for Major League Baseball, will the President and Congress impose conditions on other industries and their collective bargaining agreements?

There may be more to this than just steroids in baseball.

The President and Congress should be far more concerned with the leak of Grand Jury testimony than whether or not some player is taking "the juice" and hitting balls over the fence.

But for some reason, there is more concern about getting Major League Baseball players tested for steroids than the fact the Grand Jury testimony appeared in a newspaper.

The President spent two minutes during his State of the Union speech talking about steroid usage in Major League Baseball. For some reason, the President, McCain and others think players are role models. The truth is that players are not and never should be role models for youngsters. The players are looking for every competitive advantage available, and are no different from track and field performers, football players and other athletes who have the desire to excel. Players like Giambi took steroids and it was their choice to take the performance enhancers.

If the President and McCain really want to clean up steroid usage in sports, start in local gyms and with teenagers who feel the need to use the drugs to not only to be better in sports but also to have a better physical appearance. Start educating people with emphasis on how possessing steroids can put you in jail, and also lead to the development of all sorts of physical ailments that could lead to death.

That would be a far better solution than forcing steroid testing on Major League Baseball players, which would only be a band-aid solution. Steroid possession is illegal without a doctor's prescription. If someone has steroids in a baseball clubhouse, arrest him and send him to jail. That would send a message to everyone that baseball and society are serious about cleaning up the industry.

Steroids, Foul Territory for Congress

New York Newsday, March 15, 2005

If things go according to plan, Thursday's House Government Reform Committee hearing on steroids usage in Major League Baseball should be great entertainment but little else.

Committee Chair Tom Davis (R-Va.) says he is "not out to ruin anybody's career," but there is a need to find out what is going on in baseball. With so many seemingly more important issues facing the House—ranging from the war in Iraq to soaring gas prices to Social Security reform—it would seem that Davis's committee should be concentrating its investigation efforts elsewhere.

But not Davis and his colleagues, such as the ranking Democrat on the committee, California's Henry Waxman. They need to know why Major League Baseball has allowed the use of steroids in its workplace. Oddly enough, Davis and the committee are conducting the hearing without baseball's single-season home run record holder, Barry Bonds, on the list of people they want to question.

Davis does not want his committee's hearing to become the Barry Bonds show. Perhaps if Bonds testified, Davis's 15 minutes of fame would be diminished.

Congressional sports inquiries are often pointless. Committees conduct hearings, politicians shoot off their mouths, and it all leads nowhere. The current investigation seems particularly pointless because members of the committee have no power to order workplace changes and appear merely to be playing gotcha.

Congress has already criminalized steroids possession. So if anybody should be investigating such matters, it should be law enforcement officers. Arrest a player or two if need be. Congress should stay out of it. Saying the committee is investigating for kids' sakes is absurd.

The timing of the committee's hearing is very suspicious. It seems that Davis, Waxman and the other committee members became aware of the problem only after the release of Jose Canseco's book detailing the former outfielder's steroids usage during his career. If Davis or Waxman were so interested in baseball's steroids problem, they are rather late in showing they care.

Steroids usage was being talked about as part of the baseball culture throughout the 1990s despite the fact that Congress in 1990 passed legislation that criminalized steroids possession in the United States without medical clearance.

The issue came up during President George W. Bush's 2004 State of the Union address. Back in 1992, private citizen Bush was the managing general partner of the Texas Rangers, a team that traded for Canseco. Canseco, in his book, said Bush had to know that he and others were using steroids. The White House put out just one statement saying the then-minority owner Bush knew nothing about Canseco's claim.

If Davis really wants to get to the bottom of the steroids allegations, he should bring in the president, along with team trainers, baseball's security detail, law enforcement officials, former Commissioner Fay Vincent (who thought that cocaine use, not steroids, was the big problem when he was thrown out of his office in 1992), along with others who have been around during the entire "steroids era" to find out what they know.

Instead, the committee wants to hear from just big-name baseball players, which on the surface seems to indicate the committee is more interested in outing certain players as users than in really conducting a thorough investigation.

Just what can a Congressional committee do? Get people to testify under oath and perhaps determine if what Canseco wrote in his book is truthful.

Members can ask Commissioner Bud Selig's representative, Rob Manfred, and players association executive director Don Fehr what they know about steroids usage. They can also question former Oakland Athletics general manager Sandy Alderson, now Major League Baseball's executive vice president for baseball operations; San Diego Padres general manager Kevin Towers and seven players— Canseco, Jason Giambi, Mark McGwire, Sammy Sosa, Rafael Palmeiro, Frank Thomas and Curt Schilling.

The committee isn't writing legislation like the Sports Broadcast Act of 1961 or approving the 1966 American Football League-National Football League merger. This hearing is more on the lines of sports talk radio. The more outrageous the talk, the better it is for ratings.

Ultimately, committee members will make some statements and criticize Major League Baseball, but it's really a non-issue with both baseball fans and the voters. Baseball fans are still buying tickets and merchandise, watching the games on TV and listening on radio. They don't care. They want to know who hit the ball and how far it went and if the player was part of their fantasy pool.

A Subtle Weakening of Women's College Sports

The Orlando Sentinel, March 30, 2005

It's March-going-into-April Madness time around the college sports scene, as both the Men's and Women's NCAA College Basketball Tournaments conclude with the Final Four and Championship Games. But very quietly among all this heightened interest in college basketball, the Bush administration may have subtly weakened Title IX of the Education Amendments of 1972.

In many ways, the Title IX legislation opened the door for women in sports and other fields, including medicine and the law, because Title IX bars sex discrimination in any educational program or activity that receives federal funding, including athletics. Now that door may be shut to some women athletes.

The U.S. Department of Education, without holding any public hearings, posted on its Web site new Title IX sports guidelines. Colleges and universities can comply with the Title IX legislation by asking their female students if they are interested in playing sports by responding to e-mail surveys. If there is a lack of response to the surveys, then a school can avoid offering sports opportunities to women and be in compliance with Title IX.

It's that simple. Answer an e-mail correctly and maybe a college or a university will have a women's team available.

Maybe.

The Department of Education's edict apparently caught the NCAA by surprise as well, because NCAA President Myles Brand issued a written statement saying, "The e-mail survey clarification will not provide an adequate indicator of interest among young women to participate in college sports. Nor does it encourage young women to participate, a failure that will likely stymie the growth of women's athletics and could reverse the progress made over the last three decades."

Title IX has changed how college sports are played in the country. Before 1972, the U.S. General Accounting Office released a figure showing that 32,000 women had participated in college sports, and that figure grew to 163,000 by 1999.

Men no longer get 95 percent of the dollars earmarked for sports, and that is causing friction in the men's teams coaching fraternity. A good number of those coaches think Title IX has taken away their ability to get the best athletes for their teams because they can't spend scholarship money solely for men's teams.

Men's sports programs have been eliminated at schools. But, oddly enough, Title IX was never meant to level out the college-sports playing field and give women sports opportunities. Title IX's original intent was to give women a fair chance at being accepted in a school and for women professors to get equal opportunity at advancing within the system.

Title IX has worked. By 1994, women received 38 percent of medical degrees earned in the United States, compared with 9 percent in 1972; 43 percent of law degrees, compared with 7 percent in 1972, and 44 percent of all doctoral degrees, up from 25 percent in 1977.

Title IX is too tied into sports. And that brings a more significant question that needs to be answered. Should colleges and universities be in the big-time sports business? College sports has become a $5 billion-a-year industry, and schools are paying as much as $2 million a year for football coaches.

The Title IX argument comes down to money and who should get it for sports. Are men more deserving of the money because they take part in traditional sporting events or are women equal partners?

The answer should be that women are equals.

And do you know what else is wrong? Colleges and universities should not be farm systems for the National Football League and the National Basketball Association. They should be institutions of higher education first and foremost.

Title IX has created diversity in society and is not just a piece of sports legislation—no matter what the jocks say.

The Bush administration went after Title IX in 2002 and 2003 but backpedaled and left the provision alone. Now, the Department of Education has established new March Madness rules. For those who enjoy women's college sports, watch the games now because in a few years, a good number of women's sports teams could disappear.

Congress Should Leave NFL Alone
NBCSports.com, April 1, 2005

On the first night of spring, Carolina Panthers owner Jerry Richardson seemed a bit upset as he sat at a table looking for something to eat at the NFL owners party at the Ritz Carlton in Kapalua, Maui.

Richardson, who along with his fellow owners helped pay for the party, wanted some beef or chicken not the fish that everyone was eating but me. I had chicken that was specially prepared for me by Chef Mark. Richardson asked me where I got the chicken. I said ask Mark but he wasn't interested in waiting. Richardson then said goodbye to the people at the table leaving with his wife, presumably hungry, but he didn't seem like he was too concerned about anything that night but getting something to eat and soon.

Steroid usage by the Carolina Panthers seemed to be the farthest thing from Richardson's mind. In fact, over a four-day period in Maui, NFL owners talked about revenue sharing, extending the collective bargaining agreement, television, and high ankle sprains.

Steroids were not on the agenda.

But less than two weeks later, Richardson has a major problem as do his fellow 31 NFL owners along with Commissioner Paul Tagliabue. California Democrat Henry Waxman, after hearing that CBS was going to run a report that three Panthers players were given steroid prescriptions by a South Carolina doctor, has decided that it may be a good time to reconvene the House Committee on Government Reform and talk about steroid usage in pro football.

Committee chair, Virginia Republican Tom Davis, and Waxman, the ranking Democrat on the committee, held a hearing on March 17 about the usage of steroids in Major League Baseball after reading Jose Canseco's tell-all book.

Now Davis and Waxman plan to hold a hearing based on a CBS News report.

It's good to see Congress working on an issue like steroid usage in sports while the Iraq War continues; there is still military action in Afghanistan; when North Korea and Iran may have nuclear weapons;

and the dollar continues to slide while gas prices spike. Yet the Congressional committee wants some basic information on steroid policies from a number of sports leagues.

Davis, Waxman and the other committee members can go back to their districts and say they are working hard for their constituencies although it is hard to see how stronger testing for a banned substance, steroids, will create jobs, fund education or help people who need health benefits.

Tagliabue has been asked to appear before the same committee to testify about how football regulates the performance-enhancing substances. The committee also wants to hear from NBA Commissioner David Stern, NHL Commissioner Gary Bettman, which goes to show that at least Congress recognizes that the NHL still exists on paper, along with representatives of the NCAA, Major League Soccer and U.S. Track and Field.

Apparently Congress is not particularly worried about women's sports or the minor leagues or even high school sports and athletes using steroids on those levels. There is not enough star power to generate interest from that athletic pool.

Richardson and the NFL have known about a Drug Enforcement Administration probe of Dr. James Shortt of West Columbia, S.C. for a while. Shortt is under criminal investigation for his role in the deaths of two patients after giving them hydrogen peroxide infusions.

CBS News reported that Jeff Mitchell, Todd Sauerbrun and Todd Steussie filed prescriptions signed by Dr. Shortt for steroids in 2003 but could not say if any of the three used the banned substance which is legal when prescribed by a physician.

The three players did not test positive in the NFL's test for steroids. Waxman, citing the CBS News report, issued a statement saying that, "the reports that football players have used steroids raise important issues about the effectiveness of the NFL drug-testing policy. The committee should examine the new allegations as part of its investigation into steroid use in sports."

The NFL in a preemptive strike of its own has announced it would like to toughen its steroids drug-testing program.

Waxman was a major player in the March 17 baseball hearing, which has produced two results. Mark McGwire would not talk about possible steroid usage and that has infuriated sportswriters who vote for the Baseball Hall of Fame. *The New York Times* outed MLB's medical advisor Dr. Elliot J. Pellman for discrepancies in his educational record and professional credentials on his biography that he submitted to the Congressional committee.

Congress is not proposing any new laws based on the March 17 committee hearing nor should it. This committee should not dictate what kind of performance enhancing drug testing should be administered in sports or other professions.

There is a simple solution for steroid usage, arrest the users. Congress made the possession of anabolic steroids without medical permission illegal in 1990.

The Panthers players probe is a law enforcement case and the DEA should investigate Dr. Shortt and Richardson's Panthers players to see if there was any wrongdoing. That's where this investigation belongs, not in some room up in Capitol Hill.

Steroid Spinoff: Doctor-Patient Privacy Rights at Risk
The Orlando Sentinel, April 13, 2005

Major League Baseball has outed one player so far in the medically administered drug tests for steroids, a federally banned substance in the United States since 1990.

Tampa Bay Devil Rays outfielder Alex Sanchez tested positive for some "substance" and is sitting out a 10-game suspension. That should be troubling for American society as a whole because Sanchez along with the 41 minor-league players who have been suspended after testing positive for "something" have lost their doctor-patient privacy rights.

Now, Congress is pushing for more punishment for professional athletes if they are caught taking banned substances. This is rather unseemly behavior for Congress, because Congress should be looking to protect and strengthen doctor-patient privacy rights, not enforcing drug laws. That should be left up to law-enforcement agencies.

Sanchez claims he took something that contained a substance on baseball's banned list but is legally sold at nutritional stores. If that is the case, Congress and the U.S. Food and Drug Administration should be looking into what products are being sold at those stores, and Congress should not be conducting inquiries into the results of athletes' urine tests.

Congress and the FDA were rather slow in getting ephedra off the market, even though 155 deaths nationally were linked to its use. On December 30, 2003, the FDA issued a consumer alert on the safety of dietary supplements containing ephedra. The alert advised people to stop buying ephedra products and that the herb would be taken off the market by March 1, 2004.

In 1995, the FDA started getting complaints that weightlifters and dieters were using a product that could endanger their health. But it wasn't until after the ephedra-related death of 23-year-old Baltimore Orioles pitcher Steve Bechler on Feb. 25, 2003, that the Department of Health and Human Services, Congress and the FDA took notice.

A few House members seem so intrigued and blinded by professional sports performance-enhancing drug usage and sports celebrity that they feel there is a need to drug test athletes for all types of legal and illegal substances without due cause, usurping workers' rights and collective bargaining agreements.

Congressman Tom Davis, the Virginia Republican who heads the House Committee on Government Reform, and California's Henry Waxman, the ranking Democrat on the panel, only got interested in the topic after reading Jose Canseco's tell-all book about steroid usage in baseball during his career. Waxman's interest has grown more after he read about a CBS News report concerning a South Carolina doctor who allegedly gave steroid prescriptions to at least three Carolina Panthers football players.

Now Davis and Waxman have expanded their probe of drug testing to the NFL, NBA, NHL, NASCAR, track and field, soccer and cycling. Ironically enough, all of these professional sports leagues, except the NFL, send athletes to the Olympics, and recently the president of the International Olympic Committee, Jacques Rogge, applauded the March 17 congressional hearing on steroid usage in baseball and the need for stronger drug testing.

Is Congress pulling out all the stops to make sure New York gets the 2012 Summer Olympics by pressuring sports leagues to step up performance-enhancing drug testing?

Rogge recently said in Australia that countries that don't agree to the World Anti-Doping Agency's Olympic drug-testing won't be considered as potential Olympic hosts and that those nations could be banned from the Olympics.

New York is in the running for the 2012 Summer Olympics.

The most offensive and worrisome part about the baseball suspensions is how results were exposed, in that they were splashed all over the place in almost a gleeful manner. How many other industries are required to publicly name employees who fail drug tests?

It's wrong to go public with the results of a drug test and it's wrong to release that information to the media. There are those who argue that baseball players and other athletes—because they are role models for kids, attract massive media interest and make millions of dollars—should adhere to a different standard. But those who argue that players should be held to higher accountability have it wrong.

Politics and Baseball: Mix Well and Serve
Washington Examiner, June 29, 2005

Major League Baseball is seeking an owner for the Washington Nationals who has a high political profile.

Apparently baseball is going to get just that. Just look at the people bidding for the team.

But MLB may be entangled in a political process no one saw coming. MLB Commissioner Bud Selig and Chief Operating Officer Bob Dupuy are interviewing prospective owners and going through the process.

It should be seamless.

Except two Republican congressmen, Tom Davis of Virginia and John Sweeney of New York, are objecting to the inclusion of George Soros in Jonathan Ledecky's group. Both congressmen have suggested that MLB's 83-year-old anti-trust exemption that allows the industry to act as a monopoly could be in trouble should Ledecky's group get the approval to buy the Nationals.

Soros spent millions in 2004 in an attempt to defeat President George W. Bush in his race against John Kerry. Needless to say, Soros is not a Republican favorite. But sports owners are highly political animals. One of John Henry's partners in the Boston Red Sox ownership group is the former U.S. Senate Majority Leader George Mitchell, the Maine Democrat.

No one in Congress has ever objected to Mitchell's Red Sox ownership.

San Diego Chargers owner Alex Spanos was George W. Bush's second biggest campaign contributor in 2000 and put a lot of money into 527 attack ads against Kerry last year.

Baltimore Orioles owner Peter Angelos is a major Democratic Party supporter and donor.

San Diego Padres owner John Moores was a major Bill Clinton supporter and donor.

Rupert Murdoch owned the Los Angeles Dodgers for a while.

Former Houston Astros owner John McMullen evicted his team from the Astrodome for a month in 1992 so the Republicans could hold the party's convention in the stadium.

George W. Bush was the managing general partner of the Texas Rangers from 1989 through 1994 and one of his Rangers partners was Fred Malek, another bidder for the Nationals.

Take a look at sports ownership lists and you will find individuals of all political stripes. But their political views have not affected whether or not a league approves them as an owner. An owner's fitness is judged by his pocketbook.

Fans don't care about an owner's political views. Additionally, partisan politics takes a back seat in sports. Spanos is a major Republican donor but former Clinton White House staffer Mark Fabiani is heading Spanos' campaign to build a new football stadium in San Diego.

Congressmen Davis and Sweeney are entitled to their opinions. However, if they want to end MLB's anti-trust exemption they can find better reasons than objecting to George Soros being involved in the Nationals. Sweeney can look into how MLB owners can limit franchise movements, something that Washington experienced first hand between 1972 and 2004.

Congress does have a number of legitimate reasons to lift MLB's anti-trust exemption. The possibility of George Soros owning a piece of the Nationals is not one of them.

Just because someone is famous or makes a lot of money doesn't mean his or her doctor-patient privacy rights should go out the window.

Congress is setting a dangerous precedent by not protecting these workers' doctor-patient privacy rights. Today, it's athletes like Alex Sanchez who have lost those privacy rights; tomorrow it could be sports fans who lose their doctor-patient privacy rights if certain members of Congress continue on their current professional sports leagues drug-testing crusade.

Media

All Cable Viewers Deserve a Sporting Choice
Newsday, New York City Edition, March 8, 2002

Two tycoons originally from Cleveland are waging a battle over New York sports broadcasts that could affect the future of the cable TV industry.

In one corner, Yankee owner George Steinbrenner wants YES, his new Yankees Entertainment and Sports Network, available to all cable subscribers in the tri-state area on a basic service plan. In the other corner, Cablevision CEO Charles Dolan wants to put it on a premium channel and give his 3 million subscribers the right to choose whether they want it.

Right now, Dolan is the only cable operator who is resisting the YES Network. And Dolan is playing hardball because his Madison Square Garden Network had the Yankees' cable rights until last year. This could be Dolan's payback.

Meanwhile, Steinbrenner, DirecTV and American Satellite are taking on Dolan and Cablevision in ads that say, "Yankee Fans, too bad Cablevision doesn't offer YES Network."

I side with Dolan on this one, because I got my cable-TV bill the other day. Time Warner raised my basic service $3.04 per month without any explanation. So I called them and got a vague reply that programming costs were going up.

But I know why the costs went up. Sports programming, specifically the YES Network, which starts airing on March 19. I never had a say on whether I wanted this feature and that's wrong. I am getting tired of paying increases for cable TV due to college and professional sports. I want a choice in what programming I purchase.

But most local cable subscribers don't have any voice in whether they want ESPN, ESPN 2, ESPN Classic, ESPNews, Fox Sports Channel, Madison Square Garden Network, the NBA-AOL Sports Channel and the Yankees Entertainment and Sports Network because those networks are part of the basic package. Worse yet, we don't even know how much we pay for that programming because our cable bills are not itemized by channel.

Most cable operators abide by the theory that there are more sports fans than non-sports fans, and so they cave into the sports industry demands. Of course, the ratings tell a different story. For example, ESPN attracted just a 1.3-percent share of the cable audience in 2001 or about 900,000 homes on average nationally.

Despite very low sports ratings overall across the cable industry, YES chief executive Leo Hindrey contends that "sports belongs in basic. There are 27 regional sports networks in this country and they're all in basic."

Cable operators purchase the sports programming, pass the costs to their customers and get the complaints. The National Cable Television Association has begged cable sports networks for more than three years to slow down the money pipeline to sports.

Those cable operators should take a stand against the new six-year, $4.6-billion National Basketball Association deal with AOL-Time Warner and the Walt Disney Company's ESPN. One component of the NBA agreement with AOL-Time Warner calls for the creation of an NBA-AOL Sports Channel to air games.

Look at how the new channel will be funded. The NBA will ask cable operators for a monthly charge of 50 cents per subscriber. That means basic subscribers will be asked to chip in $6 annually for NBA games, whether they watch them or not. New York's Time Warner subscribers will get the basketball channel this fall.

Since Congress deregulated the cable industry, sports entrepreneurs operate on the principle of getting millions of dollars from cable. They do so because no one is stopping FOX, Disney or AOL-Time Warner from rolling over during contract negotiations.

The combination FOX Sports Network and MSG Network is costing most tri-state-area subscribers more than $3 a month. Dolan has put his money where his mouth is, as Cablevision does offer the MSG/FOX package in some of its locales as part of a paid sports tier or stand-alone channel. By the way, the Cablevision-owned MSG Network is no longer producing Yankee telecasts but Dolan's company is not reducing its MSG rate.

There is a simple solution. Place sports on premium channels and charge viewers the same way the HBO or Showtime or Cinemax premium packages are available. Cable subscribers should have the right to say "no" to YES.

The Price We Are Paying to See Sports on TV
The Bergen Record, June 4, 2002

It's a good thing the New Jersey Nets made their championship run this season, because if they waited one year, a good number of their fans would not have been able to see them beat Boston to advance to the NBA Finals on free TV.

Starting next year, there will be fewer NBA games on free TV, including the Conference Finals, and more on cable TV.

Sports has migrated from local free television—remember the Nets were once on Channel 9—to cable TV and is on the move again. And it's costing all of us money. NBC decided that the NBA wanted too much money for them to renew its network agreement and lost out to a combination of ESPN and AOL-Time Warner.

Cable can pay more money than network TV because it gets money from subscribers and advertisers and that's the rub for me. I don't want my NBA TV. I don't want my YES Network. I am getting tired of paying increases for cable TV because of sports programming.

Sports owners and their cable TV network partners have no regard for cable customers like you and me. They have caused most of those rate hikes because sports programming is very expensive.

We don't have any voice in whether or not we want ESPN, ESPN 2, ESPN Classic, ESPNews, Fox Sports Channel, Madison Square Garden Network, the proposed NBA TV and the Yankees Entertainment and Sports Networks because entities want to be part of the basic package.

And since most cable operators live on the theory there are more sports fans than non-sports fans, they reluctantly cave into sports demands. The ratings tell a different story. There just isn't a mass interest in ESPN and its affiliates and regional sports networks. Still, all subscribers pay for what a relative few watch.

Sports owners and network operators would be terrified to find out how many people really would pay for sports on TV.

Remember the old "I want my MTV" slogan when cable operators were saying no to the network? Those cable operators, through the National Cable Television Association, have pleaded with cable networks for more than three years now to slow down the money stream to sports leagues. It hasn't happened yet, but now should be the time.

Those cable operators should take a stand against the new National Basketball Association deal with both AOL-Time Warner and the Walt Disney Company's ESPN. It will cost consumers money. One component of the NBA agreement with AOL-Time Warner calls for the creation of an NBA-AOL Sports Channel to air games. That's all well and good for the business of both companies until one looks at how the new channel will be funded. The NBA will ask cable operators for a 50-cents-per-subscriber per month charge. That means all subscribers, whether they are basketball fans or not, will be asked to chip in $6 annually for NBA games. The cable operators will then face pressure from both the NBA and AOL-Time Warner to add that programming to its roster and, if they decide not to, AOL-Time Warner could leverage the operators by taking CNN, TNT, TBS, the Cartoon Network, or any combination of those networks away from their subscribers.

Sports teams now operate on the principle of getting truck loads of money from cable and they do so because no one is stopping FOX, Disney or AOL-Time Warner from upping the ante during negotiations with leagues, or individual teams.

ESPN, which just passed on a 20 percent rate hike to cable system operators, is charging about a $1.50 per subscriber per month, along with a 50-cents-per-month surcharge for National Football League games. My cable company, AOL-Time Warner, charges me $3.04 per month for the YES Network. The combination FOX Sports Network and Madison Square Garden is costing me $3.70 per month. When all the costs are added up, sports fans around this area are paying at least $7 a month to networks and teams. That's a bargain for sports fans, but not for those not using the service. In fact, it is a rip off for those non-sports fans.

The solution is simple. Place all sports on a premium channels and charge viewers the same way the HBO or Showtime or Cinemax packages are available.

Just do what Charles Dolan, Cablevision's chairman, suggested many years ago. Offer sports on an a la carte basis where consumers can choose what to buy. It's all about choice. And if that happens, maybe the cable audience will be so small, that local and network TV will once again be able to bid on sports making it available to all on free TV.

Local Basketball Rivalry Makes Fans Cry Foul

Newsday, New York City Edition, October 29, 2002

The NBA is fantastic! At least, that's one motto of the National Basketball Association. But many local fans may beg to differ. Take New Jersey Nets fans who live within Cablevision's territories or New York Knicks fans turned off by their team's mediocrity and the antics of Latrell Sprewell.

The season officially tips off tonight. Neither the Nets nor the Knicks have local over-the-air TV contracts. ABC Sports will broadcast only a handful of games, which could feature one of these teams down the line. The NBA has essentially become a cable-TV sport, so if you don't have cable and if you are an NBA junkie, you won't have very many opportunities to watch your favorite sport on free TV anymore.

And it's worse if you're a fan in our area. Knicks owner Charles Dolan won't cablecast any of George Steinbrenner's Nets games to his 3-million New York-area subscribers this season. The only time Cablevision subscribers will be able to see Nets games is when the Knicks play the Nets on Dolan's Madison Square Garden Network (first matchup is Dec. 17 at the Garden) or on future national cablecasts. According to NBA rules, Dolan can't black out ESPN or TNT on Cablevision.

Meanwhile, going into the season, Steinbrenner's Nets are near the top of the league and Dolan's Knicks are floundering. If Cablevision were a basketball team, it would be the Knicks. If the Knicks were an electronics store, it would be the Wiz. Dolan's three properties, Cablevision, the Knicks and the Wiz have a lot in common. They are pricey, have some good assets but are saddled with huge problems. The Knicks have high-priced players who can't play. Dolan's hockey team, the Rangers, are overpaid, overrated and are mediocre so far.

Dolan has been forced into belt-tightening because Cablevision's stock has plummeted to roughly what you would pay for two slices of pizza and a soda. Even at Manhattan prices. Dolan is closing down a number of his Wiz stores and is trying to sell off Clearview Cinemas and some of his cable TV properties, including Bravo.

Meanwhile, Steinbrenner is taking the elevator to the penthouse. His YES Network appears to be surviving even without Dolan's Cablevision subscribers. The Yankees remain baseball's most profitable team. Steinbrenner apparently will get a new arena for his basketball and hockey teams in Newark, in a deal that includes the Port Authority advancing Newark some money to build the venue. Our tolls at work, you might say.

Dolan is saddled with Madison Square Garden, the "World's Most Famous Arena," which is outdated and outmoded. His only hope of getting a new venue may come from Robert Wood Johnson IV's dream of a New York Jets stadium on Manhattan's West Side, or if the New York Olympic Committee gets both the United States Olympic Committee and the International Olympic Committee's designation to host the 2012 Summer Olympics.

Steinbrenner has had a good run with his teams lately. The Yankees came up just short against Arizona in the 2001 World Series, and the Nets came up just short against the Los Angeles Lakers in the NBA finals. The Devils are off to a good start.

Dolan's Knicks missed the playoffs last year, and his Rangers have been playoff strangers for years.

New Yorkers root for winners. When you lose, you're yesterday's news.

When the Knicks are good, you can't get a ticket and the team attracts high ratings. When the Knicks are bad, the Garden is half empty and only basketball junkies bother tuning in. Until last year's championship run, the Nets had never captured New York's interest, even though the franchise won two American Basketball Association titles in 1974 and 1976 with Dr. J. Julius Erving leading the way at Nassau Coliseum.

The Nets now have the Boss, Jason Kidd and a winning team. The Knicks have the Sprewell soap opera, highly paid mediocrities and the ability to stop the Nets from appearing on cable TV. Much to the dismay of their growing legion of would-be fans.

And that's the problem. Every regional sports network in the country is on basic cable, which means all subscribers pay for the particular service whether they want it or not. Dolan thinks consumers should have a choice.

Congress needs to re-regulate the cable industry and take that decision out of Dolan and Steinbrenner's hands. We viewers should be able to watch what we want.

In the meantime, the fight between two Cleveland native heavyweights, Dolan and Steinbrenner, continues into another sports season, with all New Yorkers on the losing end.

Fair and Balanced Solution Needed

Metro [Philly], October 26, 2003

It's good to know so many cable TV executives are looking after our pocketbooks. In September, Time Warner Cable chairman Glenn Britt told the Washington (D. C.) Metropolitan Cable Club that they should be careful about wanting cable TV de-regulation because it might actually end up costing consumers more money than they pay today and put some networks out of business. Meanwhile Cox Cable out of Atlanta is also concerned with our wallets. It seems that the company's chief executive Jim Robbins is tired of paying 32 percent of his programming costs to the Walt Disney Company's ESPN and Rupert Murdoch's FOX Sports Net which are only watched by just 8 percent of his subscribers. He wants to hold down costs for his customers and put the networks on a high-end premium channel.

Right now, 100 percent of Cox's basic cable subscribers are subsidizing what a fraction watches. In fact, some 76.7 million-cable subscribers across the United States fund ESPN and have no say in whether or not they want the network.

Welcome to Cable TV socialism. Congress would rather have cable TV socialism than socialized medicine. We, the people, don't want to collectively pay to keep down the cost of prescription drugs or health care for those who need it but we do for those who want ESPN. Sports networks like ESPN, FOX and Comcast Sports are the most costly channels on cable. In Las Vegas, Cox subscribers are paying $2.61 a month for the privilege of having ESPN and Philadelphia-area subscribers are paying roughly the same price.

Cox's deals with Disney and FOX are done soon and the company has no intention of accepting Disney's latest demands, which include annual 20-percent rate hikes, and from FOX, which wants a 35 percent increase. Cox wants to shift both to a pay tier and give their customers a choice. Those wanting ESPN and FOX would have to reach into their pocket and pay a hefty price for them. No more subsidies.

Needless to say the Cox plan is not being welcomed by ESPN and FOX because those networks stand to lose hundreds of millions of dollars if cable companies change the way they offer sports channels. Believe it or not, there is not much of a market for cable TV sports.

In fact, most cable networks get poor ratings but are financially successful because of cable TV socialism. For all the ballyhoo surrounding the FOX News Channel, its viewership is rather small. The combined ratings for FOX News, CNN and MSNBC are less than PBS' *News Hour with Jim Lehrer*, meaning Bill O'Reilly is not as much a factor as Lehrer when it comes to news. Those news channels would not exist without cable TV socialism. It's time Federal Communications Chairman Michael Powell, his five-member board and the Congress re-regulate the cable TV industry and give us fair and balanced choices. We should tell elected officials in Washington that we, not a cable operator or network, want the opportunity to decide what we want. Congress should de-regulate cable lines and let competing cable operators use those lines as the phone companies do. The competition would bring down costs.

Re-regulate the industry and let us decide. It's a fair and balanced solution to Cable TV socialism.

The Fight Over Cable Sports is Getting Batty

Newsday, New York City Edition, November 4, 2003

It's too bad that the Yankees didn't face the Cleveland Indians in the American League playoffs. Then George Steinbrenner could have challenged Cleveland owner Larry Dolan and Cablevision to a winner-takes-all competition: If the Indians lose, then the Dolan family would agree to leave the YES Network alone and place the rookie channel on Cablevision's basic roster.

And if the Yankees had played the Atlanta Braves in the World Series, then Steinbrenner could have challenged its owner, Time Warner, to leave the YES Network alone and place it on its basic lineup.

Of course, had Steinbrenner lost either series, he would have had to allow those cable television operators to do whatever they wanted with YES, which would have meant letting cable subscribers choose whether they even wanted YES.

But blame it on the Marlins, if you will. Now lawyers from Steinbrenner's YES Network will be slugging it out with Time Warner's attorneys. YES is contending Time Warner violated terms of the YES-Time Warner agreement by giving Time Warner cable subscribers a choice.

Time Warner had decided to make YES an option for its customers after Cablevision reached a truce with Steinbrenner. During the summer, a year-and-a-half after Time Warner rolled out YES (and conveniently forget to tell its subscribers that YES was being added—or that it was raising its rates by $3.04 a month for a service that was costing them $1.82 per subscriber), the giant media company informed its customers that they finally could say no to YES and get a dollar a month off their bill.

The Time Warner decision came after various New York City and state elected officials, along with those in New Jersey, pressured Steinbrenner and the Dolan family into a temporary solution that let Cablevision subscribers choose whether they wanted to watch the Yankees' 2003 season. But neither the YES Network nor the Dolans have budged from their positions, so the battle will continue before an arbitrator.

Meanwhile, another new front in the sports war has opened down south that bears watching up here. The chief executive officer of the country's fourth biggest cable operator, Cox Communications out of Atlanta, has apparently grown tired of paying 32 percent of his programming costs to the Walt Disney Company's ESPN and Rupert Murdoch's Fox Sports Net, which are only watched by just 8 percent of Cox's subscribers. Jim Robins wants to hold down costs for his customers and put the sports networks on a high-end premium channel.

Right now, 100 percent of Cox's basic cable subscribers are subsidizing what a fraction watches—at $2.61 a pop, roughly what New York area subscribers pay for the same ESPN privilege. In fact, some 76.7 million cable subscribers nationwide fund ESPN whether they want it or not.

Welcome to the multi-billion-dollar world of Cable-TV Socialism. We, the cable subscribers, are all paying for what few of us watch—ESPN, Fox News Channel, CNN, MSNBC and others—so that cable operators can hold down the costs of programming for those interested in watching those particular channels. In America, we do not collectively pay to keep down the cost of prescription drugs or health care for those who need it, but we do for those who want ESPN or Fox News.

At this point, Cox has no intention of accepting the latest demands from Disney, which include annual 20 percent rate hikes, nor from Fox, which wants a 35 percent increase. Cox wants to shift both channels to a pay tier and give all their customers a choice. Those wanting ESPN and Fox would have to reach into their pockets and pay a hefty price for them. No more subsidies.

Needless to say, the Cox plan is not being welcomed by ESPN and Fox because those networks stand to lose hundreds of millions of dollars if cable companies change the way they offer sports channels. Believe it or not, there is not much of a market for cable-TV sports. In fact, most cable networks get poor ratings but are financially successful because of cable-TV socialism. (As a point of reference, the combined ratings for Fox News, CNN and MSNBC are less than PBS' *News Hour with Jim Lehrer*, meaning Bill O'Reilly is far less a factor than Lehrer when it comes to presenting news.)

It's time the Federal Communications Commission and Congress re-regulate the cable-TV industry. Give us fair and balanced choices and let us, the subscribers not the cable operators or the networks, decide what sports, if any, we want to pay extra to watch.

Comcast Could Impact Area Fans
Metro [Philly], December 16, 2003

It is well known within the television industry that Chicago is the best sports TV market in the country, and that is where the Philadelphia-based Comcast Cable will set up shop as partners in a new regional cable TV sports network. It is possible that Comcast could use its Philadelphia, New Jersey, and Beltway properties as a launching pad to set up a national sports cable TV network. It's not as far fetched as its seems even though both Rupert Murdoch and Time Warner abandoned national sports cable network platforms in the past year, since Comcast is the biggest multiple cable systems operator in the county and the company now has some extremely powerful partners in the Tribune Company's Chicago Cubs, Jerry Reinsdorf's White Sox and Bulls along with Bill Wirtz's Blackhawks.

Comcast has 1.5 million of the Chicago area's 3.5 million subscribers and will offer those subscribers the new network starting next October. Will those 2 million subscribers ever get the new channel?

The answer to that question could be the most significant aspect in whether or not Comcast will remain a regional player or go national. Planning a new cable TV sports network is a lot easier than actually getting cable operators to put it on their systems. All Reinsdorf, Wirtz and the Tribune Company need to do is ask George Steinbrenner about his problems in New York and New Jersey in getting the YES Network onto Cablevision systems, or check with Carl Pohlad in Minnesota to see how many of the big cable systems in the Upper Midwest are taking Pohlad's new Victory Sports Network which began operations on October 31.

The Chicago sports owners could call National Football League Commissioner Paul Tagliabue for a progress report on the new NFL Network, a programming service that has been designed for basic cable TV yet is only seen on DirecTV, a satellite service.

The cable TV climate has changed. Operators no longer count on sports as an important component of their business. Cablevision lost just 40,000 subscribers in the New York area when it did not show YES Network Yankees games in 2002. Meanwhile, the YES Network has filed an anti-trust lawsuit against Time Warner because that cable company changed the terms of its agreement with YES and gave some Time Warner customers the option of not taking the YES Network. Pohlad is giving his product away until the spring, hoping Upper Midwest systems operators take his channel.

In New Orleans, Cox Cable, the nation's fourth largest multiple systems operator, could not get its local sports channel on other area cable systems' expanded basic package and had to settle for an optional digital platform, which means customers had a choice in whether they wanted the Cox package in certain parts of the New Orleans market. It's a bit ironic in that Cox, the program supplier in this case, wants its customers to have a choice in whether or not they want ESPN instead of having the Disney sports channel as part of expanded basic service.

The new Chicago sports channel faces a number of problems, starting with pricing and the lack of room on basic cable. Are Chicago cable system operators ready to pay more than $2 a month per subscriber for the product and where will the network be placed? Will it be a basic, a pay or a digital channel? And will Philadelphia area Comcast subscribers pay more if their cable operator ultimately decides to compete with the biggest kid on the block, ESPN?

Thank Cable for Sox-Yanks Signings
Metro, January 6, 2004

As the Red Sox play catch up with the Yankees in a game of can-you-top-this in baseball's off-season, Red Sox fans should be thanking Rep. Edward Markey of Malden for his help in making the spending spree possible. It was Rep. Markey—the ranking Democrat on the House Telecommunications and Internet subcommittee—who thought it was a good idea for the New England Sports Network to become a part of expanded basic cable instead of being offered as a pay tier service for New England area cable subscribers.

Apparently that is where Red Sox owner John Henry and his partners are getting money to pay very high sums of cash to their baseball players or in an attempt to get the best player in the game, Alex Rodriguez.

The Red Sox are merely keeping up to George Steinbrenner's Yankees by signing the best players available and, like George, John Henry is purchasing players with money generated by NESN. Steinbrenner gets a good portion of his money from the YES cable TV network. Neither the Red Sox nor the Yankees has a new and shining facility loaded with club seats and luxury boxes, but both have tremendous corporate support and they have the bank, the cable TV network. In fact, in Henry's case, NESN is far more valuable than either the Red Sox or Fenway Park. It's a cash cow.

While the arms build up in Fenway and the Bronx is good for the Red Sox-Yankees rivalry, it's not good for the overall health of the baseball industry if you believe competition is the key to growing the sport. Milwaukee and Pittsburgh have thrown in the towel and aren't competing or even making a pretense. The Pirates sold off some of the team's better players last summer and the Brewers have said goodbye to Richie Sexson and will bid a fond adieu to the team's other high priced players. Those teams don't own cable TV networks and cannot compete with the Yankees and Red Sox.

So while Red Sox fans and even Yankees fans should be sending thank you notes to Rep. Edward Markey, people in Pittsburgh, Cincinnati, Milwaukee, Oakland, Kansas City and all the other cities where teams cannot compete with John Henry and George Steinbrenner should not only be writing to Rep. Markey but to the other 434 House and 100 Senate members. Congress needs to change cable TV laws and re-regulate the industry so that consumers have a choice in what they want to purchase for their entertainment.

Sports owners and networks don't want choice because they know the people who would actually subscribe to expensive sports channels would be a fraction of what they have now and that would mean far less revenue for people like John Henry. So if the Red Sox do win this year, Rep. Markey should be in the running for the Most Valuable Player because he and his colleagues have provided the wherewithal for John Henry to spend other people's money on his baseball team.

Trappings Take Over Pro Sports
Metro [Philly], February 11, 2004

Should NBA Commissioner David Stern have to deal with the fallout of the Super Bowl half time Show? The answer should be no. It is unfair to have Stern assume the position of moral guardian and censor and sanitize the weekend's events surrounding the NBA All-Star Game in Los Angeles. But Stern will be forced into that position and he will have to accept that responsibility because his sport, along with the rest of the industry, has brought the scrutiny onto itself.

More scrutiny will be coming later today when the House of Representatives Subcommittee on Telecommunications and the Internet holds its broadcast decency hearing and calls NFL Commissioner Paul Tagliabue to testify. Michigan Republican and committee chair Fred Upton has proposed legislation that would impose a $275,000 fine on violating indecency rules. Presumably, Tagliabue has been summoned to tell what he knows about the now infamous Super Bowl half time show featuring Janet Jackson and Justin Timberlake.

It was the NBA's competitor, the American Basketball Association, that really wedded sports with entertainment. Sure football games featured marching bands as part of a half time show along with cheerleaders and the NFL held a Super Bowl party on the Queen Mary prior to Super Bowl VII, but it was the Denver Nuggets that came up with a plan that featured singers Glen Campbell and Charlie Rich as the pre-game concert and a slam dunk contest at half time for the 1976 American Basketball Association All-Star Game. The Nuggets were worried that they could not sell out with just a basketball game, changing the very nature of how sports is presented. By giving more entertainment, they could bring in casual fans, those who choose going to a sporting event over a movie or a club.

Throughout Stern's 20-year tenure as NBA Commissioner, the league has moved from presenting just a game to a show complete with piped in music and crowd noise. It's become a meeting place, as one owner put it, for the "parent (who) is there to see the smile on the kid's face, not a jump shot. The buddies (who) are there to check out the girls and drink."

More than a quarter of a century later, today's sports owners seem more intent on marketing every aspect of their industry except for the main reason people are interested in sports. The game.

The ABA's scheme to get a few extra thousand fans to buy tickets to see some of the greatest talent basketball had to offer in 1976 led by Julius Erving, David Thompson and George Gervin has finally come back to haunt all of sports and has culminated with the pre-planned half time incident.

By the way, a marginal talent like Timberlake is part of the Walt Disney Company-NBA entertainment marriage as he has written the NBA's theme song for Disney's ABC-NBA telecasts. Both Disney and the NBA think Timberlake can drive people to watch basketball games.

Do sports promoters realize that the game is their product? Their sole product? The answer seems to be no which is why Stern is on the hot seat because the NBA and sports can't afford another Timberlake-Janet Jackson incident.

Group May Change Baseball Without Trying
Metro Weekend, May 7–9, 2004

Can the Concerned Women for America (CWA) do what Baseball Commissioner Bud Selig and the majority of his fellow owners could not do? Take George Steinbrenner's cable TV money away from him and the New York Yankees?

It seems inconceivable that a conservative group which claims to be the nation's largest public policy women's organization could end the free spending Yankees ways, but the group's lobbying efforts in Congress could change the very nature of how cable TV operates in the country.

The Concerned Women for America along with the Parents Television Council, the Consumers Union and the Consumer Federation of America have petitioned Congress and want pro choice when it comes to cable television options.

The CWA is throwing its weight behind the Video Programming Choice and Decency Act of 2004, which would give all cable subscribers the right to pick and choose what programming they want.

The bill would allow customers to pick what they want instead of having the cable company decide what is best for the consumer. For sports networks and owners that could be devastating because most people aren't sports fans and would drop sports channels, which they are currently forced to take.

Congress and the FCC have fingerprints all over sports. By not regulating cable television, both have contributed to skyrocketing player costs in baseball, hockey and basketball.

Congress and the FCC have given monopoly powers to the cable industry; cable networks including the Walt Disney Company's ESPN, Rupert Murdoch's FOX Sports Network and AOL-Time Warner's Turner Sports have spent an enormous amount of "other people's money" buying professional baseball, hockey, basketball and college games for programming on their various sports networks.

The New York Yankees-owned cable YES Network produces more money than the bottom seven local cable television contracts combined. That gives the Yankees a financial advantage over those teams which, for a variety of reasons, cannot compete with the Yankees. Which is why Selig and company have been trying to get their hands on Steinbrenner's local largesse.

"Basic cable" subscribers are footing the bill for sports salaries without knowing it. The 76.7 million basic-cable subscribers are paying at least $3 billion in annual fees to subsidize both professional and college sports. Because of deregulation, Congress and the FCC have crafted a system that has created a bank for sports and has left consumers with no choices and no rights.

The CWA wants control over what it considers cable TV indecencies.

And by accident, they may change how major league sports is financed in this country, which may be a frightful thought in sports executive board rooms across the country.

Cable's Monopoly Burns Viewers

Metro [NY], August 9, 2004

New York Mets fans who are Time Warner cable television subscribers have every reason to be irate.

They have lost the ability to watch their baseball team because of a dispute between Cablevision and the cable company. In a nutshell, Time Warner is refusing to pay more money for Cablevision's Madison Square Garden, FOX Sports New York and Metro channels.

It seems the cable consumer can do nothing while the cable multiple systems operators and the cable networks fight over money. And the truth is, if a consumer wants cable, that consumer has to deal with a government-sanctioned monopoly.

There are no choices because Congress and the Federal Communications Commission refuse to change cable rules and give consumers choices when it comes to selecting what networks they want. But that may change sometime in 2005.

On November 18, the Federal Communications Commission will hand in its report to the House Energy and Commerce Committee on cable television pricing. Already, one of the FCC Commissioners, Michael Copps, is indicating that he may be ready to give cable subscribers a choice.

"It obviously sounds attractive. It gives consumers options. That's always something we ought to be looking at," Copps recently said. "Obviously, consumers don't like to pay for something they don't watch or don't really want."

Should the FCC recommend that cable TV be made available on a per-channel basis to consumers and Congress implements changes, cable subscribers would reap the financial benefits, and cable operators and the cable-TV-sports industry would be greatly affected. Consumers would pay only for what they want to purchase and not subsidize channels they don't want.

Cable operators and networks are dead-set against any kind of cable re-regulation, claiming that some networks would have to charge subscribers more money for their favorite channel and that other channels, which are bundled into one large cable-price group, would cease to exist because there just aren't enough people watching their programming.

Virtually every one of cable's 76.7 million subscribers gets ESPN, but if ESPN were offered on an a la carte menu, just how many people would take the service? Maybe a tenth? Maybe less? It's an answer ESPN's owner—Disney—doesn't want not to know.

Cable TV should become like PBS and provide programming that appeals to consumers and get those customers to want to pay monthly programming costs.

Mets fans who are Time Warner subscribers should have a choice in whether or not they want the games, not the cable operator. But sports and cable-industry executives shouldn't be worrying yet. Congress just doesn't have any appetite to change the way Americans get their cable TV.

Messing with the Pigskin:
NFL Could Throw Networks for a Loss
Newsday, New York City Edition, September 9, 2004

Attention, Giants and Jets fans as well as tailgaters and couch potatoes everywhere. Enjoy it while you can. The National Football League is about to change your routines beginning in 2006, and that could affect what you wear, what you eat and drink, and how you enjoy the sport.

So, as the season kicks off tonight (with the Jets and Giants hitting the gridiron this Sunday), you ought to know that the NFL's broadcast and cable TV contracts will end after the 2005 season—and nothing will ever be the same.

In 1998, the NFL inked an eight-year, $18-billion-deal with Rupert Murdoch's Fox, Viacom's CBS and Walt Disney's ABC-ESPN combination. While the deal has been a financial windfall for the 30, then 31 and now 32 NFL owners, it has not been a gold mine for the networks—some claim they've lost hundreds of millions of dollars.

The team owners want more than a token pay raise from the networks, while the networks are trying to figure out just how valuable the NFL really is to them. The league left CBS behind in 1994 and signed deals with Murdoch, General Electric's NBC, Turner Sports' TNT and Disney's ABC-ESPN. But such was the power of football that the NFL made Fox a real player.

Ten years later, the NFL is more of a loss leader. Yes, it remains the best sports vehicle for advertisers to reach young men, but there is no sizzle to *Monday Night Football* anymore, even with John Madden in the booth. Sunday's audiences aren't growing, and that is a big concern for both Fox and CBS in the upcoming contract negotiations.

So changes are in the offing. Could *Monday Night Football*, a fixture on ABC since 1970, end up on ESPN? ABC is losing millions of dollars on the production, and a switch to ESPN—with its smaller audience but ability to charge subscribers and advertisers to fund the program—could occur.

Some of the more radical ideas floating around include starting the season in mid-to-late September, which would mean playing the conference championships and the Super Bowl in February.

Now that change in schedule would be significant. The Super Bowl has already become a February affair, but the conference championships haven't been. February is one of TV's sweeps month, when the networks use the ratings from their programming to set advertising rates. A Super Bowl is a ratings winner; championship games are big numbers grabbers as well. The NFL could force networks to ante up more money if the league's crown jewels are shown then.

Of course, it means New York football fans who venture out to the Meadowlands could be exposed to Green Bay-like conditions or worse on game day. Bad weather combined with a poor win-loss record could mean many empty seats before the regular season ends. That would be the trade-off for NFL owners.

Of course, if the Jets somehow manage to get their West Side stadium built, fans may not have to worry about the weather after the 2008 season—those games would be indoors. On the other hand, there would be no more tailgating, because there won't be an outdoor stadium parking lot—and that's half the reason many show up in the first place.

Meanwhile, NFL owners are also considering starting Sunday games later, say at 2 and 5 o'clock Eastern Time. It would play havoc with the networks' prime-time programming if games ended after 8 p.m.. Would the networks go along with that? Another NFL idea is creating a Thursday-night package to bring in more dollars for what is now an off night. But that would take a game away from Sunday football broadcasts. Would the Sunday rights holders then pay less?

There are other pressing questions that need answers. Will the league remain at 32 teams and shift a team in a weak TV market, such as Indianapolis or New Orleans, to Los Angeles? Or will the NFL add a team to L.A. in 2008 and thus diminish the owners' individual share of the TV revenue? Will cable's NFL Network get any live games?

In many ways, the NFL's next TV contract is going to change the popularity of the sport. Fans may have to rearrange their workweek and Sunday schedules and even their winter vacations. Two years from now, football is going to be quite different for tailgaters and couch potatoes alike—it's something that they may want to tackle today.

League's Roots in TV
Metro, September 29, 2004

The National Football League doesn't highlight the date of Sept. 30, 1961 but that was the day that the modern NFL was born.

On that day President John F. Kennedy signed the 1961 Sports Broadcast Act, which allowed the National Football League to prosper.

Simply, Kennedy's signature allowed National Football League Commissioner Pete Rozelle to bundle the 14 NFL franchises' TV rights into a league package and sell all league games to one network. Rozelle landed a deal with CBS, which was worth far more money than what each team would get individually and that changed how pro football operated.

According to *Forbes Magazine,* Wellington Mara's New York Giants franchise is worth $692 million. Woody Johnson's Jets are slightly less valuable, at $685 million.

Both play at an old facility, Giants Stadium. If the Jets ever move to the West Side of Manhattan, the team might match or come close to the NFL's most valuable team. According to *Forbes,* the Washington Redskins, Daniel Snyder's team, is worth more than a billion dollars.

If Mara gets a renovated Meadowlands facility, he and Bob Tisch would probably see their investment escalate to Redskins dollars.

When three big market owners went along with Rozelle back in 1960 and 1961 and gave up their individual TV rights, they agreed to some-thing that has been called "league think," a concept that put the needs of the NFL ahead of the desires of individual team owners.

Rozelle was able to drive up the price for TV contracts by playing NBC off against CBS. NBC in 1965 decided to sign a deal with the rival American Football League, which gave the new league almost equal dollars to the established NFL. By 1966, the two rivals merged once again working together to maximize TV revenue.

Television dollars have been the foundation to the riches. The 32 owners share the massive TV contracts equally.

Unlike baseball, NFL owners rarely complain about losing money. "League think" is the reason why football has become a social event for some and a moneymaker for NFL owners and players.

TV Money Could Back '05 NBA Lockout
Metro Weekend, October 8–10, 2004

NBA teams are getting ready for the season but basketball fans should be aware of this. The league could lockout its players on July 1, 2005 and the owners will still be getting cable TV rights fees from the Walt Disney Company which, according to David Stern, plans to pay the league whether there are games being played or not.

Don't expect ESPN to lower its rates to 86 million-plus cable and satellite subscribers should there be no NBA. ESPN and the various regional cable TV sports networks around the country didn't bother to refund money during labor disputes in the past and won't start now.

There seems to be no incentive for big cable companies like Comcast, which owns the 76ers, or Cablevision, the owner of the New York Knicks, as well as numerous other owners with TV connections to offer rebates to their customers for missing games. Cable is a government-regulated monopoly with few, if any, rules designed to protect the consumer.

NBA owners will be getting paid by cable TV customers to help prop up a lockout should it come to pass. And NBA owners could go that way. They want to make changes in guaranteed contracts, keep the luxury tax and possibly push for a minimum age entry rule. The players would like to see the luxury tax disappear and teams bid for free agents without fear of excessive taxation.

In 1998–99, NBA owners got guaranteed TV money from NBC to fund their lockout. This time don't be surprised if it's Disney behind a work stoppage.

TV Money is Key to Success
Metro, October 14, 2004

The American League Championship Series featuring the New York Yankees and Boston Red Sox accentuates exactly what is right and what is wrong about Major League Baseball.

The Yankees, with a glorious history, and the Red Sox, whose fans feel cursed, are showcase teams in showcase markets.

The Yankees-Red Sox rivalry is no doubt making FOX happy because that network will get better than expected ratings with the two old and bitter rivals. But the Yankees-Red Sox series also proves that teams don't need a new stadium to compete at the highest level.

What teams really need are their own cable TV regional sports channels. In 1988, the Madison Square Garden Network partnered with the Yankees in an effort to keep that TV outlet viable 12 months a year.

That money made the Yankees baseball's top revenue team. Later the Yankees further increased their cash flow by creating a network of their own, YES.

The Red Sox and the Boston Bruins have been partners in the New England Sports Network for 20 years. It was the cable network, not the Red Sox nor Fenway Park, that drove up the bidding to the $700 million price tag by the team's current ownership group.

They got a cable TV network, which is increasingly becoming baseball's answer to financial problems.

The success of the Yankees and the Red Sox is forcing baseball owners to rethink their business models.

The Mets Fred Wilpon is walking away from a lucrative contract with the MSG Network for a chance at even more money with a Mets Network backed by two cable giants, Comcast and Time Warner, starting in 2006.

Cable TV is now the bank and its revenue is uncapped. That's why the Yankees and Red Sox have the best players and are competing annually for a championship and why small market teams can only hope to catch lightning in a bottle and compete for a couple of years.

Policy Malfunction. FCC Looking to Lay a Hit on Violence in Televised Sports
Northern Virginia Journal, October 20, 2004

Attention FCC Commissioner Michael Powell and your fellow Commissioners along with Congressional members.

Lighten up!

Get a DVD of *Slapshot* and have some fun and don't worry about hockey fights. People seem to enjoy a good fight every once in a while or more.

After all Super Bowl Sunday is a national holiday and what is more violent than a football game?

Commissioner Powell and his colleagues may have to rule rather soon on whether or not a hockey game that features fights is suitable programming between 6 a.m. and 10 p.m. daily.

The Federal Communications Commission is doing a study at the behest of Congress on over-the-air, cable and satellite television violence and how that type of programming impacts children.

If the FCC comes up with new rules that include sports violence, the showing of NHL games on TV could be shoved back into a late nighttime slot after children's bedtimes.

The FCC already has rules banning so-called indecent programming on radio and TV between 6 a.m. and 10 p.m. daily. The FCC indecency guidelines have been in effect since 2001 but most people were unaware of the rules until this year's Super Bowl when Janet Jackson's bare breast was exposed after a "costume malfunction."

Viacom, which owns CBS the network that presented the 2004 Super Bowl, was fined $550,000 for broadcasting the incident.

Hockey fighting might very well be considered violent programming. This is a major problem for not only the National Hockey League, but also the National Football League, which has sold violence for decades going back to the CBS production of "The Violent World of Sam Huff," narrated by Walter Cronkite, in 1960.

One of sports' major selling points is violence. When the Nashville Predators began marketing its product to Tennessee in 1998, the marketing department showed hockey collisions and NASCAR accidents in sales presentations.

Sports TV highlight shows feature collisions, fighting and general rowdy behavior. Sports video games routinely feature fighting and blood.

The National Hockey League is fighting back. Last Friday, NHL attorney Phillip Hochberg wrote a letter to the FCC saying that "the NHL feels that it is improper to even consider whether a sport like hockey would fall into any definition of televised violence."

Should both Congress and the FCC get involved and regulate fighting in hockey, violence in football, boxing matches, and high and tight pitches in baseball?

Can Congress and the five FCC Commissioners really push hockey and other sports contests into the so-called off hours, and would sports fans, advertisers and sports owners along with network executives go along with it?

And does a hockey fight really lead children into violent behavior?

After all millions grew up watching *The Three Stooges* which really featured violence. Did the Stooges really affect kids growing up? Of course not. And will the FCC stop at sports, or the Stooges or Bugs Bunny, and will local TV News also be relegated to the 10 p.m. to 6 a.m. graveyard shift?

The Congress and the FCC should be concentrating on real issues.

And if people don't like a program, just change the channel. It's that simple.

Comcast's Roberts' Control Over Sports

Metro [Philly], October 23, 2004

Brian Roberts just might be the most powerful man in sports. If you don't think the Comcast CEO isn't, consider this. Comcast is starting its fourth regional sports network in central California and this sports network could have a profound impact on the futures of the Sacramento Kings and possibly the San Francisco Giants and the Oakland Athletics.

Comcast's California network starts just after a new regional network based in Chicago that features the Cubs, White Sox, and Bulls, and when the National Hockey League returns, the Blackhawks began. Roberts has also partnered with Charter Cable and the Memphis Grizzlies for a Tennessee area network and with Time Warner in a New York network featuring the Mets in 2006.

Roberts, head of the Flyers and 76ers parent company, is no doubt supporting NHL Commissioner Gary Bettman's lockout strategy and will be a voice in determining whether or not the NBA imposes a lockout on its players next July. Roberts is so powerful that he can order rebates to all of his customers who are paying for a product they aren't getting at the moment—NHL hockey—and all the other sports networks would have to go along with the edict.

Roberts is partners with ESPN and the FOX Sports Net. Roberts' Comcast is also partners with the NHL's Washington Capitals and Chicago Blachkawks along with the NBA's Washington Wizards, Chicago Bulls and Sacramento Kings. Roberts actually helps control the budgets of his competitors.

Roberts also has deals with the NFL to carry its new network and has an Atlanta Falcons and a Dallas Cowboys channel on various Comcast systems.

How could Roberts become the most important man in the future of the Sacramento Kings NBA franchise? The Kings owners, the Maloof brothers, want a new arena in Sacramento and negotiations have bogged down. The Kings have had no local cable TV contract to speak of until Roberts stepped in and used his 700,000 central California cable subscribers as a base for Comcast SportsNet West that will cover a 350-mile territory that stretches from Visalia and

Fresno north to include the greater Modesto, Stockton, Sacramento, and Chico areas. Robert's network's coverage area will expand into the Bay Area to include San Francisco by January.

Roberts is giving the Maloofs one of the three basics that an owner needs to be successful. A strong local cable TV contract. The Maloofs now have more money that could possibly be used for a new Sacramento building for Maloof's Kings and WMBA's Monarchs.

The Kings give Roberts a strong anchor program to build a network around, but the real key here is getting into San Francisco and possibly getting the Oakland A's or Giants as part of the network. A network needs year round programming anchors and an NBA team along with a Major League Baseball team pretty much assures a network is viable.

Roberts has the money, he has the delivery system and the clout. The cable guy from Philadelphia may be the most powerful man in sports.

Cable Helps Mets Reach for the Stars
New York Newsday, February 4, 2005

"Meet the Mets, Meet the Mets!" should be the name of a new television series, because the New York Metropolitans are hotter than a reality TV show—especially when you consider what's going on behind the scenes.

As everybody knows, when you produce a TV show, you gotta have stars, which is why the Mets have shelled out almost $200 million to bring in Pedro Martinez, Carlos Beltran and re-up Kris Benson, or rather his wife Anna, a popular Howard Stern guest. (Last December she was voted *FHM Magazine's* sexiest baseball wife.) How convenient that Anna Benson also wants to be the star of her own reality TV series.

The Mets ceased being just an overpriced baseball team last spring when owner Fred Wilpon terminated his cable TV contract with Charles Dolan and Cablevision's Madison Square Garden Network and decided to put together his own deal. In 2006, Wilpon, along with Time Warner and Comcast, will debut a Mets regional sports network.

Ironically, this year Dolan will be the beneficiary of the Mets' hiring Martinez and Beltran, because his network figures to pick up a significant number of viewers—at least early in the season—and he can raise his advertising rates accordingly.

Dolan won't get any additional fees from cable subscribers. He gets that money whether one person or 500,000 people watch Mets games on MSG or Fox Sports New York. It doesn't matter because the Federal Communications Commission and Congress won't let cable subscribers choose what channels they do or don't want—and that won't change in George W. Bush's second term.

Cable TV makes strange bedfellows because Wilpon's new television partners are involved with rival baseball teams. Time Warner owns the Atlanta Braves, the Mets' National League East nemesis, while Comcast Cable is TV partners with the Philadelphia Phillies, another perennial competitor. Does that mean that Time Warner, which now has a significant interest in the Mets, wouldn't mind seeing the Braves' domination finally end? After all, the better the Mets are, the more advertising money flows into Time Warner's wallets.

Comcast doesn't own the Phillies—it just cablecasts some of their games—but it is a full partner with the Tribune Company's Chicago Cubs, the White Sox, the Bulls and the Blackhawks in a Chicago regional sports network. What would be better for Comcast's coffers? A stronger Mets team, a winning Cubs team or a tougher Phillies team?

At least George Steinbrenner doesn't have that problem with the YES Network. He has sole star power all right, but he only has distribution partnerships with Comcast and Time Warner. Still, that brings up an interesting question. What if Steinbrenner's costs become out of line for Comcast and Time Warner and the two companies, as owners of the new Mets network, decide to pull Steinbrenner off their systems? That would kill his golden goose and probably threaten the Yankees' dominance.

Oh, what a tangled web.

These days Major League Baseball is less about sports and more like a series of complex business transactions. Take New York's second or third most compelling team (depending on whom you root for), the Boston Red Sox. The Sox, partly owned by *The New York Times*, are also in the cable TV business, thanks to the Red Sox New England Sports Network, one of Comcast's offerings in New England.

As the Mets are about ready to enter the stratosphere, Fred Wilpon will join George Steinbrenner in acting like a New York baseball owner with money to spend. The Mets organization needs big names, big stars, to move its product in this media market—something Steinbrenner learned a long time ago.

So, life won't get any easier for small-market baseball franchises like Kris Benson's old team, the Pittsburgh Pirates. They will still have to find talented young (cheap) players, develop them and hope they can hang onto them for five years before trading them to teams like the Yankees and Mets for future prospects. And, if you are Steinbrenner and Wilpon, who needs scouting? They have cable TV and can buy just about any player they want, especially if they need to give their "reality baseball show" a boost.

Stadiums

Giuliani Shouldn't Play for the Teams
Newsday City Edition, May 2, 2001

Just whom is Rudy Giuliani kidding? The New York City mayor is in his final months of the job and he is still seeking new, taxpayer-subsidized baseball parks for the New York Yankees and New York Mets. Was Giuliani serious when he said that neither the Mets nor the Yankees would be financially able to compete with Atlanta, Baltimore and Boston in the distant future for players and playoff spots without new stadiums now? Yankees owner George Steinbrenner is planning to get more than $100 million in annual TV rights fees at some point in the next few years now that he is free of his Madison Square Garden Networks commitment.

The Mets, despite a stadium that is now 37 years old, were the second highest revenue-producing team in 1999, raking in $132 million behind Steinbrenner's Yankees, who pulled in $175 million. Steinbrenner could have sold the Yankees for $600 million even though the House That Ruth Built is 78 years old. New York teams will always get huge TV contracts because of our area's large population and financial wherewithal. It's a fact of life.

But Giuliani wants to go ahead with his plan to provide new revenue-producing facilities for both teams. His problem? He needs New York State as well as the teams to kick in financially. And he needs to sell the notion to city residents that two profitable Major League Baseball teams need still more money and that some of it would have to come from city coffers.

It's an even tougher sell because of the economic slowdown. Giuliani has asked city departments for 2-percent budget cuts and is planning for 6-percent reductions in next year's budget if the economy doesn't pick up.

Giuliani is also dealing with problems such as failing schools and rising wage demands from public employees. Still, he wants the ballparks as well as a new football/Olympic complex on Manhattan's West Side, a new Madison Square Garden and a venue that could host the NCAA Final Four and other attractions.

If that doesn't work out, there are reports that a new Yankee Stadium would be built on city land next to the old stadium in the Bronx.

One of the Mets' co-owners, Nelson Doubleday, doesn't necessarily want a new stadium and would settle for a refurbished Shea Stadium. His partner, Fred Wilpon, is more amenable to the mayor's idea.

New stadiums mean fresh revenue streams. Teams use new ballparks as an excuse to raise ticket prices and create high-priced club seats along with more luxury boxes. Wider concourses allow more people to stand on concession lines and spend more money for beer, hot dogs, yearbooks and whatever else teams sell. It all brings in more revenue.

"There is a good chance that we will be able to work things out with the Mets and the Yankees," said the mayor, who has been a Yankee fan for life, at a press conference on opening day. "We are talking to them on a consistent basis and I have been in involved in some of the [talks]. I think there is a good chance we can work that out." Giuliani wants the parks, but his reason for spending billions of dollars through a public-private industry partnership just doesn't mesh with the economic facts.

"The reality is, as I have said many times, both of them need new ballparks in order to be competitive," said the mayor. "Maybe not this very year, but in order to be competitive over the next 10, 15, 20 years with their major competitors. Boston is getting a new ballpark; Baltimore has a new ballpark.

Atlanta has a brand new ballpark. That's all going to enhance their revenues.

And if the Yankees and the Mets want to remain competitive with Baltimore, Boston or Atlanta, then that's something we just have to do." Yes, Atlanta does have a fairly new park, Turner Field, which opened in 1997, but the Braves' parent company, AOL-Time Warner, has cut its workforce by 10 percent across the board. Boston is going nowhere with its bid for a new ballpark to replace Fenway. Baltimore's Camden Yards is in its second decade of use.

Despite Giuliani's best attempts at painting a poor financial future for the Mets and Yankees, it's inaccurate. The Yankees are charging $65 per loge seat on game day and $55 for a seat in the main box. Mets ticket prices are also very high, with prices ranging from $12–$43. Both teams can get top dollar for their product because there is plenty of corporate support available. TV money is plentiful as well. Fan support is high-when the teams win. New York's baseball franchises have the money they need. So just whom is Rudy Giuliani kidding?

Confronting Difficult Arena Questions
The Bergen Record, July 16, 2002

A state senate has embarked on yet another arena debate—a debate that has taken place in Minnesota, Missouri, Connecticut, Florida, Texas, Arizona, Illinois, Pennsylvania, New York and, yes, even in Trenton.

The issue is basic, should government pitch in with public tax dollars to help pay for a venue that will exclusively be used by a private business?

The question may be simple, but the answer is far more complex. In fact, there has never been a real answer other than it may be good for civic pride to have Major League Baseball, the NFL, an NBA or NHL, or MLS, or even a minor league team in a particular area.

New Jersey has the biggest financial stake in a proposed Newark arena project that would house the Nets and Devils. The state would issue $165 million in bonds that would be repaid with sales and income taxes collected from a special "sports and entertainment" district that would be created around the arena site. The YankeeNets would pay $120 million and Newark and Essex County would put up $50 million. All of that is predicated on the project's being built on time and on budget.

If the senate committee does its homework and asks the right questions, the Senate may have a unique opportunity to get answers that have eluded municipalities, sports teams and taxpayers.

Is government spending on stadiums and arenas worth the cost or should government get out of the sports business? All the Senate needs to do during its three scheduled public hearings on whether or not to build the Newark Arena is to put emotions aside and ask some very basic, but difficult questions of both sides.

In the late 1990's in Louisville, Kentucky, attorney J. Bruce Miller spearheaded the campaign to build an arena to attract an NBA team. Louisville could not come up with the political wherewithal to spend some $250 million in taxpayers' money to build an arena.

Miller took the anti-stadium/arena lobby to task, contending that stadium/arena building is a good way to help a local economy.

The "millions upon millions of dollars that are spent to construct such arena/stadia are not 'lost in thin air' or evaporated into the Milky Way. They are used to paying American contractors and businesses of all kinds—all of whom, in turn, pay wages/salaries to tens of thousands of Americans who use that money to support their families and to pay taxes back to the very governments who facilitate the "exchange.""

But Miller's argument doesn't make much sense to an economist like Andrew Zimbalist, the author of *Sports, Jobs and Taxes: The Economic Impact of Sports, Teams and Stadiums*.

"By Miller's reckoning," he said, "all any city would have to do is hire contractors to dig a hole and then hire other ones to fill it and we'd have thousands of construction jobs, income and tax payments. Voilà, no more unemployment. Not so easy unfortunately.

"Where does the money come from to pay the diggers? Taxes, directly or indirectly (via debt service) higher taxes mean more public and less private spending. That's the beginning of the story."

Zimbalist's beginning is where the senators should take their hearings. Will the arena just make more money for George Steinbrenner and the rest of the YankeeNets group or will the arena be the first step in generating new revenues, raising property values, and creating full time, non minimum wage jobs?

Arenas generally don't create good jobs. Most of the arena jobs are per diem and don't even pay minimum wage. According to former Nashville Mayor and one time New Jersey resident Phil Bredesan, who tried to persuade Devils owner John Mc Mullen to move his hockey team to Nashville in 1995, he would have been better off building a supermarket than a football stadium and an arena; a supermarket might generate more money and jobs, but it just isn't a source of civic pride.

Is a proposed Newark Arena a lightning rod that will boost both the city and state's economy or will it just pump more money into YankeeNets and become some sort of symbol of civic pride. The legislators need to ask that question and then make an educated, not emotional, decision on whether sports funding is appropriate.

Footing the Bill for Sports Stadiums
Bergen Record, May 9, 2003

Apparently the Newark Arena plan isn't dead yet. That's no surprise because municipalities never give up in their attempt to either become or maintain big league status. Newark isn't a big league city, but New Jersey is a big league state and eventually someone will come up with a solution that will satisfy Newark, the YankeeNets, George Steinbrenner, Gov. McGreevey, Mayor Sharpe James, and others.

But there are some underlying questions that need to be answered even before one shovel is placed into the ground in Newark or the renovators start work at the Meadowlands Arena. Will the Newark arena be on the city's property tax roles and will the real cost of the construction ever be known? Whatever the initial price tag on the building or renovating project, it doesn't include paying off the debt service on bonds. Will the occupants of the new or renovated arena pay property taxes or the debt service or does that become the responsibility of Newark, Bergen County, and ultimately New Jersey residents?

New Jersey isn't alone in its desire to build arenas despite the large budget deficits. Virginia plans to make an offer to Major League Baseball to build a baseball park in order to bring the Montreal Expos to Northern Virginia. The estimated cost to build the stadium is $400 million and that is already 33 percent higher than it was in 1996.

Virginia politicians seem to be ready to open the vault despite the fact that the state is one of 44 in the country with a large budget gap.

New Jersey residents visiting Virginia and using local hotels or motels will contribute to that stadium, if it is ever built. Part of Virginia's stadium funding plan includes a hotel-motel room tax. It's a taxation without representation scheme because travelers have no say in what they pay in local hotel-motel room tax. It's an underhanded way of raising money for private industry but it's the way municipalities have been operating for more than 15 years to keep or gain "major league" status.

From Arizona to Florida, to Texas, to the state of Washington and many other places around the country, taxes that should have gone for municipal services, schools, and senior citizen programs have funded stadiums. And speaking of taxes, most of the sports arenas and stadiums around the county don't pay property taxes to their local municipalities.

It's all part of the game politicians play to appease sports owners.

In the Seattle area, the car rental tax was 8 percent in 1992. In 1998, the car rental tax was 18 percent. Where did the money from the extra funding go? Most of it went to building a new baseball park, a new football stadium, and for a renovation of the city's indoor arena.

But before anyone in New Jersey commits money to any arena, a review of Detroit's problems is in order. Detroit just announced that it would have to close 16 public schools to close a $100 million budget deficit. This is the same city that, along with the local county and the state of Michigan, kicked in about $320 million to build a baseball park that opened in 2000 and a football stadium that opened last fall.

The Tigers have been pitiful and the novelty of a new ballpark complete with all sorts of so-called fan-friendly gadgets (which is a code word for significant price hikes for tickets and concessions along with parking), wore off quickly. The Lions will sell out because football is more of a social event than a game. But how much money does football really bring into a community? At most, the Lions will play two pre-season, eight regular, and two playoff games over a 365-day period.

Yes, Detroit did get the 2006 Super Bowl and the NFL claim of generating about $300 million in spending during Super Bowl week. But even if the NFL is correct about the economic impact, that doesn't help Detroit-area students or some of their teachers who will lose their jobs in 2003.

New Jersey politicians better have the answers to hard questions before they sink taxpayers' money into an arena to maintain "big league" status.

New York Experiencing a Widespread Change of Venue
Metro, May 17, 2004

Baseball Commissioner Bud Selig is stadium hunting in New York. During the Yankees' last trip west, while addressing Oakland's desire for a new stadium in the Bay Area, Selig let Governor George Pataki and Mayor Michael Bloomberg know that "the Mets need a new stadium and they believe they need a new stadium."

Here's some advice for Bud and Mets owner Fred Wilpon. Take a number.

The New York metropolitan area is about ready to see the biggest and most costly plans ever to build or renovate stadiums and arenas for the Giants, Jets, Nets and Devils, with the Islanders, Knicks, Rangers, Yankees and Mets not far behind.

If everything goes according to plan, the Devils will end up in Newark using monies advanced to Newark by the Port Authority in a new arena. The Nets will move to Brooklyn using Bruce Ratner's money and municipal dollars for infrastructure, the Giants and New Jersey will renovate Giants Stadium and New York City and State will kick in $600 million for Woody Johnson's Jets Stadium on the West Side of Manhattan.

Just how Woody and the Jets slipped ahead of George Steinbrenner and Fred Wilpon is a bit of a mystery in the stadium game. Steinbrenner was supposed to move his Yankees to that coveted west side location under a plan first considered by the Governor Mario Cuomo in 1993.

Wilpon's Ebbets Field II plans were unveiled in the late 1990s. But neither project gained any traction although the city gives both Steinbrenner and Wilpon a $5 million a year through 2006 for "research and development" of a new stadium.

Johnson may have been able to forge ahead because he is a major Republican fundraiser in a state with a Republican governor and a city with a Republican mayor.

Mount Vernon Mayor Ernie Davis is attempting to cobble together a money package to build an arena right off the New Haven

Metro North line. The midsize arena would be home to three mid level NCAA basketball teams, Iona, Fordham and Manhattan.

Yonkers, which has a fiscally challenged school system, wants to use public funds to build a small stadium and business complex to house an independent league baseball team. Islanders owner Charles Wang is interested in building a new home for his hockey team and possibly go after an NBA team. But Nassau County has budget issues.

With all of the planning for all the new places, there is a question that needs to be addressed. Is the area saturated with too many teams and too few events? These arenas and stadiums go after the same circuses, wrestling shows, concerts, tractor pulls, ice shows and kids fare. Just how are any of these buildings, which for the most part are funded by tax dollars, going to make money? There are too many buildings now. Yes, Fred Wilpon thinks his Mets need a new stadium, but so does everyone else and that is a major problem for taxpayers.

NYC Should Turn Eye Toward New Orleans
Metro, June 1, 2004

Here's a question for Governor George Pataki, Mayor Michael
Bloomberg, Deputy Mayor Dan Doctoroff and New York Jets owner
Robert Wood Johnson IV.

Have you been following what is going on in Baton Rouge
and New Orleans in the saga of the New Orleans Saints' money
guarantees? If not, everyone connected with the West Side stadium
project, both for and against, should be paying close attention
because what is happening in Louisiana could happen here.

The Saints' tale goes back some four years when team owner Tom
Benson began to complain that his one time money-producing lease
at the Superdome was falling way behind other franchises because
other cities and states were underwriting costs for sports facilities and
then giving most of the stadium's revenue streams away to grateful
owners.

The owners claimed they needed the money to be competitive
and the cities claimed that the stadiums were economic engines
even though an NFL team will only play 12 games a year at a given
facility.

Benson did what any respectable owner would do. He threatened
to leave town without a new stadium. Benson's options were limited;
San Antonio had a relatively new stadium but was a very small
market like New Orleans. Los Angeles had just lost an expansion
franchise and there was no stadium on the horizon.

Louisiana didn't have money on hand for a new stadium, but
Governor Mike Foster and the legislature eventually cut a deal. They
would give Benson handouts as a thank you for not moving. The first
check was for $12 million in July 2002, the next check was for $13
million the following July.

The Saints' owner would get his money from a combination of
sources which included money from sales taxes hikes on hotel and
motel rooms and naming rights to the Superdome. All seemed to be
settled in 2001. But the events of September 11 occurred, tourism
dropped off and New Orleans hasn't recovered.

The Superdome remains the Superdome as no corporation has bought the naming rights.

Louisiana has just $7.9 million of the $15 million due on July 5 and state officials have no idea how to make up the difference. They are hoping Benson will renegotiate the 2001 deal. If Benson doesn't get his money on July 5, he can void the agreement by Sept. 18 and shop his franchise to other cities that might be more grateful that an NFL owner wants to place his business in their burg.

Benson was to get about $186 million overall in state handouts. The Saints' owner is due $15 million on July 5, 2005 then $20 million in 2006 and 2007; and $23.5 million in 2008, 2009 and 2010.

Louisiana was going to renovate the three-decades-old facility over a two-year period in 2006 and 2007 by raising the tobacco tax, and combining that with a hike in the hotel-motel tax in Orleans and Jefferson parishes or an increase of the sales tax in New Orleans.

Benson's story should be a precautionary tale for those here in New York pushing for the West Side stadium. Make sure you have the money at hand and don't make outrageous promises or your football owner can shop his team around when you default on your promises.

Teams Finding Stadiums Outdated After 20 Years, Sometimes Sooner
Metro, July 26, 2004

For sports fans who think stadiums are baseball cathedrals, the news out of Miami that the city's arena is up for auction should make them take notice.

Stadiums and arenas aren't hallowed grounds, just replaceable gathering places.

The Miami Arena was built with public funds and opened in 1988. Within two years, NBA Commissioner David Stern was wondering out loud why his league bothered to put a team in an inadequate arena that lacked luxury boxes and high-end seating. The Miami Heat moved into a new building in 1998 and the Florida Panthers were gone by 2000.

Today, the Miami Arena website still lists upcoming events but there is a ribbon that runs across the site screaming out. "The Miami Arena, former home of the Miami Heat and Florida Panthers, will be auctioned off on August 10, 2004 in "as is" condition. The minimum purchase price is $25,000,100. The auction will be organized by Fisher Auction Co., Inc. of Pompano Beach, Florida."

For $25 million, one hundred dollars someone can own a useless structure that will have to be razed by the highest bidder.

The Miami Arena is where Pat Riley coached basketball, where Bill Torrey built an expansion hockey team into a Stanley Cup finalist. Yet its fate is pretty much sealed. The site where the arena is located is currently zoned "C1-Restricted Commercial but allows for 300 multifamily units per acre."

Whoever ends up with the 16-year-old arena well might get back the investment by building a combination of commercial and residential properties.

How does this relate to New York? Sports arenas and stadiums have a limited shelf life. In the 1980s, then Baseball Commissioner Peter Ueberroth recommended that no team sign more than a 20-year stadium lease with any city. All of the stadiums built in the late 1980s and early 1990s like Camden Yards are entering their middle age phase. A stadium now lasts about 20 years not 50 or 60 or 100 years. The new places have a high burn rate.

And they aren't economic magnets. In Seattle, two new ballparks haven't brought new business to the stadium area. In Nashville, there isn't much development around the new football stadium. It's hard to believe a new Yankee Stadium or Shea Stadium will be an economic engine in the Bronx or Queens or that a Jets Stadium will revitalize the West Side.

Charlotte is bidding goodbye to its Coliseum next spring after 17 years. All of these places seem to go out the same way. Some company comes in, wires the structure with explosives, then brings down the building. The Miami Arena will probably meet the same fate. It's something that politicians should consider before putting up billions for sports stadiums and arenas. It's not sacred ground, it's just a building where sports operate.

Sports Owners Profit from Tax Deals Like the Garden's
Newsday, August 3, 2004

It is rather fitting that President George W. Bush is being renominated in a sports arena that has not paid any property taxes or its Con Edison electric bill in more than two decades.

Bush will get the nod at Madison Square Garden, which in the early 1980s (when it was owned by Gulf and Western) somehow persuaded Mayor Ed Koch and members of the City Council that the Knicks and Rangers would move elsewhere without a property tax exemption. Today that exemption is worth about $12 million annually.

Considering where the Knicks and the Rangers end up each season, perhaps the teams could use the money they save on taxes to invest in players who will make them better. After all, the teams are our investment, too.

Bush, himself, owes his political career to his sports investments. He spent $600,000 to buy a piece of the Texas Rangers in 1989 after selling his shares in Harken Energy for about $750,000 to a still unnamed buyer.

Subsequently Bush became the team's general managing partner, but there was some question as to just what his role was. Once, when I was at spring training, an American League owner told me that "George thinks he's important, but little does he realize that all he does is shake hands."

Early in Bush's tenure, he threatened to move the Rangers to St. Petersburg, Fla., unless Arlington, Texas, gave the owners' group a new taxpayer-funded stadium. Arlington eventually approved a sales tax hike to pay for the new facility and got the land for it through eminent domain.

Bush may have played a part in the 1992 baseball coup d'état when the owners fired Commissioner Fay Vincent. Bush reportedly wanted to be the next commissioner but his fellow owners suggested he pursue politics instead. One of the owners, Bud Selig, made himself commissioner.

Despite being on the campaign trail in 1994, Bush must have had a say in that year's devastating baseball strike. Federal Judge Sonia Sotomayer ended the labor action in March 1995, after determining that the baseball owners, including Bush, had not bargained in good faith. (Incidentally, Judge Sotomayer was appointed to the bench by Bush's father.)

Bush's years as Rangers owner lasted from 1989–98. He won the governor's race in 1994, defeating Ann Richards. Four years later, Bush walked away with a $13.4-million profit when the club was sold to Tom Hicks.

As Bush showed, owners need local mayors, governors, city councils and state legislatures to buy into the notion that the teams need new stadiums in order to survive, and more often than not the politicians have come up with stadiums built on the public dime.

Owners need corporate support to buy the big-ticket items, luxury boxes and club seating. Those seats become tax write-offs for corporations. And you know those big salaries that the owners pay their players? Well, they can depreciate the contracts much like you can depreciate a car on your tax return. And new tax codes pending in Congress promise to give the owners even more.

The Republican National Committee seems to have no problems with holding its convention in an arena that doesn't pay its fair share of property taxes, which could be allocated to any number of pressing budget items. It's no big deal to the CEO of the 2004 Republican Convention, Bill Harris, that the Garden's owners from Gulf and Western to Chuck Dolan have picked up over $200 million in subsidies.

"We were invited to come to New York City by the civic, business and labor leaders," Harris said recently at the New York Press Club in Manhattan. "They proposed the site and we are very happy with it."

He added, "We are here conducting what we consider very important business for the nation actually. We think it will be very helpful to New York City and we are very happy they offered the package they did."

Harris said the Republicans received the same type of package that New York would offer to any sports franchise. The party got an arena and resources to help pay for transportation and the renovation of the building. In effect, New York is paying for the privilege of having Republican convention delegates in town.

Meanwhile, street vendors too will pay, as they will be kicked off the streets around the Garden. Ken Mehlman, the Bush-Cheney 2004 campaign manager, has said that he hopes those people understand that the convention is important. The vendors are about ready to find out what the true meaning of "compassionate conservatism" really is.

The Rangers and Knicks fans will just have to wait a little longer for their relief.

During Florida Cleanup, Forget Sports
The Orlando Sentinel, September 14, 2004

You would hope that smart men like George Steinbrenner, Rich DeVos, Larry Dolan, John Swofford and Jeffrey Loria would start to realize that life doesn't start and end at sports. But it may take more than a few hurricanes for people like Steinbrenner, DeVos, Dolan, Swofford and Loria, along with a minority of people who follow sports, to get the concept that sports is just a diversion. It's just not that important compared to weathering a hurricane and dealing with a storm's aftermath.

Yet, when things return to normal, people will start wondering whether or not DeVos wants to keep his basketball team in Orlando or the Citrus Bowl should be renovated. Sure, a sports franchise or a championship football game is something that some people in a community can boast about, but that's about it.

It's not life or death.

Which is why people like Steinbrenner need to be singled out. Steinbrenner, a Tampa resident and New York Yankees owner, belittled the Tampa Bay Devil Rays organization for not forcing its players to go to New York to play a baseball game last week because Devil Rays officials thought their players should stay at their homes with their families during Frances.

DeVos wants a new arena for his Magic in Orlando, but with all the devastation, can DeVos really ask city and county officials for money to build an arena for a sports franchise? Dolan, the Cleveland Indians owner, is looking for a new spring-training home either in Winter Haven or elsewhere. It doesn't matter to Dolan where he winds up. He wants to go where he can get the most money. The question is: Will Winter Haven have the type of money needed after the storms to keep the Indians?

Cleveland lost its spring-training home when Hurricane Andrew wiped out Homestead back in 1992. Homestead lost baseball, but life went on as the town attempted to rebuild and Florida changed building codes statewide. Baseball and the Indians seemed rather unimportant.

Swofford, the Atlantic Coast Conference Commissioner, recently put up his conference championship game for bid, encouraging nine cities, including Orlando, to make the conference an offer. Swofford just wanted the money, and, like Dolan, he wanted to go where he could get the most money for a one-day affair.

The ACC didn't go to Orlando because its football stadium doesn't match up with Jacksonville's facility.

Hurricanes Charley, Frances and now Ivan should put the sports world on notice that sports is just an entertainment forum and that the real world doesn't revolve around Tracy McGrady being unhappy as a member of the Orlando Magic. The real world doesn't revolve around an aging stadium like the Citrus Bowl or an arena that is maybe used by its anchor tenant at most 60 times a year under the right circumstances.

For most people, their lives didn't change after the Tampa Bay Buccaneers won the Super Bowl or the Tampa Bay Lightning won the Stanley Cup. It's not the real world.

No, the real world is people cleaning up after Charley and Frances and preparing for Ivan. The federal government, meaning all Americans, will be paying for some of the cleanup around the state. Florida taxpayers will absorb some of the cost as well, and that leaves the question: Where is all of that money coming from?

There should be no money left in the till for sports projects at this point and owners should not be asking Florida officials for handouts. There is no way Tallahassee politicians should even consider funding a baseball stadium in Miami for Loria and his Marlins, nor should Orlando officials or state politicians open the coffers for DeVos, and Tallahassee officials should not consider funding Dolan's spring-training dream facility.

There is too much that needs to be done for Floridians who have been twice devastated and face a third round of destructive weather. If that means that DeVos takes his basketball team to Kansas City, that's the way the ball bounces. If Loria leaves Florida for some other spot, Miami will survive and so will Jupiter, where Loria's team trains for the season. If Dolan doesn't like Winter Haven anymore, that's too bad.

The reality is that sports isn't real life, Florida has to get back on its feet, people need to return to their jobs and the state has to rebuild. That rebuilding should not include sports.

Getting Olympics Won't Be a Slam Dunk
Newsday, November 2, 2004

It's hard work to bring the 2012 Olympics here because New York has to pass a global test.

No matter who wins the presidency, New York faces an uphill battle to get the Games. After all, Old Europe gets to vote on what city should host the event. And Old Europe has an entry in this race: Paris. The City of Light appears to be the favorite in a close contest that also includes Tony Blair's London, Madrid and Moscow.

The International Olympic Committee will award the 2012 Games on July 6, 2005. So the New York Olympic Committee (a/k/a NYC2012) has just nine months to persuade more than 100 countries that New York is the perfect place to hold an Olympics. The outcome of the election could be pivotal.

Many of the IOC voting members come from countries that have problems with the present administration on numerous issues from rejecting the Kyoto Treaty to the Iraq War. Those countries' members on the IOC could summarily dismiss New York's bid not on the details of its proposal, but on their perception of our government's policies.

In the Olympics, choosing a host city is not necessarily based on merit. In the past, IOC voters have acted like a coalition of the bribed, the coerced, the bought and the extorted when it comes to selecting a host city. In 1999, the IOC acknowledged that some IOC members had acted "inappropriately" in the bidding process when Salt Lake City landed the 2002 Winter Olympics

Some say our international reputation won't have anything to do with the final decision. They note that Vancouver will host the 2010 Winter Olympics and claim that the IOC will not award a continent consecutive Olympics. But that theory isn't true, as Athens hosted the 2004 Summer Games and Turin, Italy, has the 2006 Winter Games. Another notion making the rounds is that New York won't get the 2012 Summer Games because the United States has hosted the Olympics four times since 1980. But that shouldn't be a deal breaker when you consider how much money American television, General

Electric's NBC Universal unit in particular, is giving to the IOC for the broadcast rights to the 2010 and 2012 events.

NBC would prefer to show the Games in real time in the United States, which is what Vancouver and New York can offer. Money talks in sports, especially in Olympic bidding.

The list of five finalists is instructive. Paris was an IOC favorite before the Iraq war and remains that way. The United States and the United Kingdom were, of course, the only coalition partners who fought in it. France, Germany and Russia were opposed.

The Olympics are more than an athletic competition. The Games are a corporate bazaar where multi-national businesses show off their products in a 17-day advertising campaign that is televised worldwide. The Olympics also provide a political platform for those who are looking to air their grievances.

Should President Bush be re-elected, next July's IOC vote could be a highly charged and emotional decision because of the Bush administration's dealings with Iraq. Look what has happened in the United Nations already regarding our foreign policy in the Middle East. Passing the IOC's global test won't be any easier.

Ever the optimists, the New York Olympic Committee, Gov. George Pataki, Mayor Michael Bloomberg and Deputy Mayor Dan Doctoroff, the real force behind the bid, believe that the city has the best chance of landing the Games. But they may find out that politics and international diplomacy—and not a strong plan—are much more important to IOC members when the final vote is taken. And those voters from Old Europe may come to feel that the Games would be a perfect fit on the left bank: the left bank of the Seine.

Your Tax Dollars for D.C. Stadium
The Orlando Sentinel, December 7, 2004

If you think big government spending in Washington, D.C. is limited to just Congress, you are wrong. Washington Mayor Anthony Williams wants to break all sorts of spending records on building a baseball park for the Washington Nationals team that starts to play in 2005.

And people in Orlando, including Mayor Buddy Dyer, should take note of what is going on in Washington because it is conceivable that federal dollars will be going into a project that is being built for private industry.

Cities and municipalities are once again spending record amounts of money to build sports arenas and stadiums. Kansas City is building an arena that could house an NBA team in 2007, a team like the Orlando Magic. Arlington, Texas, is putting up $350 million to help fund the Dallas Cowboys' new stadium that will open in 2009. New York may spend billions to fund two baseball stadiums for the Mets and Yankees, a West Side stadium for the Jets and the 2012 Olympics, and a Brooklyn arena for the New Jersey Nets. Even Wichita, Kan., is in the act, putting up public money for a major-league arena in a small town.

The Washington baseball stadium is a budget breaker. Originally, Mayor Williams thought the stadium would cost about $440 million, and he would get the money by taxing Washington businesses that had more than $3 million in gross receipts, and collecting rent from the baseball team. But a closer look at costs revealed that Williams and his staff underestimated costs and that the stadium project may cost the district $614 million should it ever get built. And it's a stadium most people in Washington don't want built.

The stadium plan would include upgrades of Metro stations near the ballpark and monies from that would come from the district along with Maryland and Virginia. Other funds for infrastructure could come from federal coffers, which means people from Central Florida would kick in money for a Washington stadium.

Stadiums and arenas are playpens for athletes, but not local residents who can never use the super recreational facility. Still, future athletes have to start training somewhere, and this is where Mayor Williams and Mayor Dyer, who wants to upgrade the current Orlando arena and upgrade the Citrus Bowl, have a problem.

Budgets are tight everywhere in the country, and one of the first line items checked for fat is recreation. Usually those programs are slashed in small but significant ways. Repairs at local recreation facilities for little things like seesaw repair or just cleaning up garbage from an area might be delayed or not ever occur because there is no money left in a budget. Schools also cut out athletic programs, and there is a growing trend nationally to have junior and senior high-school students pay to play because there isn't enough money to fund sports programs or art and music programs.

Yet politicians always seem to find money for major-league sports.

Mayors, city council members, governors and other elected officials have fallen in love with the idea that a sports team somehow makes an area complete, even though most people cannot afford to see more than one or two Major League Baseball, NBA, NHL or NFL games a year.

Politicians put forth excuses as to why they spend hundreds of millions of dollars on big-time sports. Charlotte Mayor Pat McCrory came up with a reason that his city is spending $240 million on a new arena for an NBA expansion team.

"Every night, your score is given on TV, it puts you in the big leagues as far as drawing attention to your city, and we think the Bobcats will do that."

It's an interesting theory, but does having a sports team attract other major businesses to the community? The answer is probably not. Studies have indicated that Charlotte did not gain businesses in the 1990s just because it had an NBA expansion team, the Hornets, and an NFL expansion team, the Panthers. In fact the Hornets left three years ago for a better arena deal in New Orleans.

It would be hard to believe Mayor Dyer using that reasoning as well. The Orlando area is an international destination because of the area's theme parks. But in 1997, then-Nashville Mayor Phil Bredesen told me that he went after the NFL's Houston Oilers and an NHL expansion team to give Nashville more exposure even though

Nashville is internationally known as the Country Music Capital of the World.

Politicians should have better reasons than having a score read on TV to give millions to fund a sports arena that may have minor economic benefits in a small area—especially if that funding comes at the expense of recreation, educational or health programs.

Fans, Beware. The Price of Big-Time Sports Hits You Where You Live

Newsday, New York Edition, January 4, 2005

If there were a New York sports commissar, that exalted ruler would soon be delivering the annual state of our sports address. It would be both a warning cry and a rallying call for fans who have been on the receiving end of some hard knocks lately. It would go something like this:

My fellow New Yorkers, these are trying times for the sports fan. Two U.S. senators want to impose steroid testing on Major League Baseball players because of a drug scandal in the game that includes two Yankees, Jason Giambi and Gary Sheffield. It is apparently more important to Arizona Republican John McCain and North Dakota Democrat Byron Dorgan that Major League Baseball Players are clean than that the mess in Iraq, the soaring deficit and the falling dollar are dealt with.

But I digress. Hockey fans may soon be an endangered species. National Hockey League owners have locked out their players since last year because of what they say are soaring deficits and the need for cost certainty. But basketball fans could face the same fate. National Basketball Association Commissioner David Stern and his 30 owners could lock out their players as early as July 1, which doesn't bode well for those who derive income from Rangers and Knicks games at the Garden.

Money is the name of the game, no matter what the game is. Even though the Yankees and Mets continue to spend big bucks for pitchers like Randy Johnson and Pedro Martinez, Major League Baseball owners say they are still looking at ways of cutting payrolls and sharing more revenues to make teams in Milwaukee, Pittsburgh and Cincinnati more competitive with us. The small-market owners want a piece of the Yankees' and Mets' cable-TV revenue pie. But our own George Steinbrenner and Fred Wilpon may not want to be very generous. They haven't won a World Series in a while, have they? So the pressure for "cost certainty" may fall on the players, and that means that a baseball lockout may be on the horizon in 2007.

Last Sunday the Jets may have gotten a free pass into the playoffs, but the odds of their playing in the Super Bowl look about as long as their chances of playing in a new West Side stadium. Jets owner

Woody Johnson will take Manhattan, but not the Bronx or Staten Island. If he doesn't get his way, it's conceivable that the Jets could end up in Los Angeles. The National Football League wants a gridiron team in the nation's second largest market by 2009—and coincidentally the Jets' lease at the Meadowlands ends in 2008. And speaking of that Jersey swamp, the Giants want a new stadium there to replace their 28-year-old facility. Meanwhile, the Devils, assuming they hit the ice again, are moving to Newark, and the Nets may move to a new basketball arena in Brooklyn.

And let's not forget that Steinbrenner and Wilpon want new ballparks, too.

My fellow citizens, it's incumbent upon us to raise taxes to build all of these new facilities. It's good for us economically because stadiums are supposedly economic engines that revitalize an area. Sure, some critics will point out that Cleveland spent hundreds of millions of dollars on a baseball park, a football stadium, an indoor arena, and the Rock and Roll Hall of Fame, and that city still ranks among the poorest in the nation. And some may say that a large supermarket has more of an economic impact than a colossal stadium, but we want our teams to be competitive.

We need big-time sports.

We need the 2012 Summer Olympics here because New York City Deputy Mayor Dan Doctoroff decided many years ago that New York should host a two-week sports fest. The Olympics will cost billions, and that could leave us with billions of dollars of debt and tie up the city with construction for years and years—all so that some athlete like Ben Johnson can win a gold medal and then have it stripped from him because he failed a drug test. It's good for us to host the Games.

We need to spend public money on sports—even if we have to cut education and social services and raise transit fares—so that sports owners can get more revenues from the sale of luxury boxes to high rollers. We hope you understand that this will require some sacrifices. Fans will have to endure lockouts, and everyone will have to cough up more to pay for higher taxes and cable-TV fees. We are doing all this so that someday soon we will have a baseball, football, basketball or hockey champion in our town again. After all, we deserve it.

The Sport of Stadium Building
Bergen Record, August 16, 2005

There is a big catch in the way sports stadiums and arenas are now being funded. In case you haven't noticed, taxpayers are no longer being asked to subsidize stadiums and arenas for professional sports franchises. That's the good news for New Jersey residents as soccer's MetroStars and the NFL Giants are planning new stadiums.

But there is some bad news for taxpayers too.

Politicians and sports owners are no longer using the argument that a football stadium or an indoor arena will serve as an economic engine and will be the linchpin of financial development. Instead, politicians and sports owners are much more sophisticated in their approach to building new sports facilities.

An individual owner will build a new stadium or arena, paying for the facility out of his or her own pocket. The owner also wants acres upon acres of land complete with tax breaks and incentives such as making payments in lieu of taxes to build what sports owners now term an "urban village."

That's exactly what Major League Soccer's MetroStars are doing in Harrison and what New York Jets owner Woody Johnson had originally envisioned at Manhattan's Hudson Yards and now in the Meadowlands. Build a stadium and then build retail and office space along with housing and entertainment facilities in a compact area.

Sports used to be all about games, but the simple truth is that sports ownership looks at actual games as just a byproduct of a growing industry that includes media and real estate.

The Boston Red Sox ownership group cannot replace Fenway Park, so they are buying out real estate in the area surrounding the old ballyard and turning the area into an "urban village" complete with nightlife.

The Oakland A's owner Lewis Wolff is thinking of building a stadium near the Oakland-Alameda Sports Complex in an area that is presently a flea market. Wolff wants to build a small ballpark by Major League Baseball standards with about 32,000 seats. But Wolff's ballpark would be revolutionary. He wants to build condos into the park's outfield stands and he wants Oakland to give him acres upon acres of land so he can develop some sort of upscale business and residential area.

All Wolff needs is Oakland to give him the land and tax breaks along with federal dollars to build or fix up interchanges on I-880 and build a Bay Area Rapid Transit station and he is set to go.

In St. Louis, the Cardinals ownership is putting up most of the money for a new ballpark that will open in April 2006. But the Cardinals have become a real estate holding company and are creating "Ballpark Village," which will include retail, entertainment, office, and residential facilities.

It is still too early to tell what the MetroStars owners and what may happen at the Meadowlands, but whatever the development, it will come at a price for New Jersey residents. The Giants and maybe the Jets will get valuable land for virtually nothing and will get every tax break imaginable.

New Jersey will be on the hook for "infrastructure" costs, which includes putting in new roads, sewers and water mains. The state will minimize the risks for the owners and then trot out statistics showing just how much of an economic impact having sports teams has for a community.

Politicians will claim it is a win-win situation for everyone. The New Jersey Nets are moving to Brooklyn in a real estate deal. Bruce Ratner will build an arena and then an urban village complete with skyscrapers surrounding the new Brooklyn Arena. All Ratner wants is the land and tax breaks and incentives.

And if Ratner doesn't get all the land he needs he can always get New York City to seize land through eminent domain, and the Supreme Court has given its blessing to eminent domain seizures, to make sure he gets everything he needs to build his urban village.

Taxpayers are not being asked to pay for stadiums. The Giants, maybe the Jets, the Nets, the Yankees and Mets owners are putting up money for their new playpens. But taxpayers aren't off the hook; they will be paying for other aspects of the sports business. After all this is sports where a catch is very important.

Olympics

S.F. Wants the Olympics. The Question is Why

The San Francisco Examiner, September 2, 2001

As a New Yorker vacationing in San Francisco, my eye caught an *Examiner* headline last Friday: "Games: S.F. has a shot." The 2012 Olympics. San Francisco thinks it can host it. The headline was strikingly similar to New York City newspaper headlines of about a month ago.

At that time, I had one questions: Why are Rudolph Giuliani and New York business leaders wining and dining members of the U.S. Olympic Committee? Why would Giuliani and New York's captains of business and industry go after something that won't be staged for another 11 years, the 2012 Summer Olympics? Why bother?

Willie Brown and other Bay Area leaders should be asking the same question.

The committee is on a summer tour of New York, Los Angeles, San Francisco, Dallas, Houston, Cincinnati, Baltimore/Washington and Tampa/St. Petersburg to see if any of those cities is capable of handling an Olympics—an event that may have very well outlived its usefulness.

The committee is checking venues, housing, transportation and how cities plan to fund this multibillion dollar extravaganza. Funding is the key to the operation. The games are more than a decade away and no one has a crystal ball, so it may be tough to factor in inflation, taxes, military threats, ecological disasters and other unforeseen events.

The New York Olympic Committee would have to spend billions of dollars for new facilities such as an Olympic (or Jets football) Stadium, an indoor arena and other venues, as well as infrastructure and housing. The committee may also need to turn to the state for help. It might even have to get some cooperation from New Jersey in its bid.

The 2012 Olympics doesn't seem to be a big issue with any of Giuliani's potential replacements—Mark Green, Alan Hevesti, Fernando Ferrer, Michael Bloomberg, Herman Badillo or Peter Vallone—and that could be a problem for Olympics backers. Those candidates seem more interested in education, parks, lifeguards, affordable housing and mass transit.

Giuliani and the business leaders must know the Olympics selection process has been corrupt. There was the vote buying scandal in Salt Lake City. Atlanta organizers knew that some International Olympic Committee members were "sleaze bags" who could sell their votes, according to a U.S. Olympic Committee report in 1999. The same report also found evidence of vote-rigging in Toronto's bid for the 1996 Olympics.

The Olympics costs taxpayers millions of dollars yet never lives up to local businesses expectations. Even so, politicians and business leaders still go after the Olympics like sailors on extended leave go after companionship in port.

Everyone knows the selection system is problematic, but there was Sen. John McCain, R-Ariz, threatening to strip the International Olympic Committee of its U.S. tax exemption, limit tax deductions of international committee sponsors and direct Olympic TV revenue into the U.S. committee. The Senate Banking Committee had a bill that would extend the federal Corrupt Practices Act to include the bribing of Olympic officials.

Of course, it was all bluster. McCain's legislation never left the committee. The Olympics are the Olympics after all. It's a chance to spread international good will through sports—and who wants to mess with that?

But why does any city want the inarguably huge headlines and relatively minimal financial benefits of hosting the Olympics?

David Simon, president of the Los Angeles 2012 Bid Committee, defended his city's attempt. "The 1984 Games were organized privately, without the use of taxpayer dollars and generated a profit of $235 million" in 1984 dollars, he told me. 'The games also were an economic boon to the local area, with an estimated impact of $3 billion."

"Beyond the question of finances, the 1984 Games were enormously popular in Los Angeles," he insisted. "They proved to be a unifying force for the community to rally around, and they provided hundreds of thousands of local residents with the once-in-a-lifetime opportunity to experience the Olympics as employees, volunteers or spectators. The games were widely considered to be one of—if not the—greatest events in the city's history."

The Los Angeles Olympics were successful because the International Olympic Committee bent its rules. It was desperate to put on a good show in America because the past wasn't a pretty picture. The United States had boycotted the 1980 Moscow Games, and the 1976 Games had featured a boycott by African countries. In 1972, there was the Munich Massacre.

Los Angeles was not required to build a new Olympic stadium. In fact, the local committee constructed only one new venue. Costs were kept down purposely and the games did make money—but only because the city didn't have to build anything.

"I don't presume to speak for the other U.S. cities bidding for the 2012 Olympic Games, but on behalf of Los Angeles we have no problem determining that the Games are worth pursuing in the future,' Simon said.

The International Olympics Committee, feeling some heat, made some cosmetic changes in the selection process and barred its representatives from visiting the cities bidding on future games.

Despite allegations of recent scandals and the threat of congressional intervention, the mad scramble for the 2012 Games has begun. Why?

"New York is big and it should be the biggest and the best," said former Gov. Mario Cuomo. "Everything that's big, everything that's worthwhile, New York should go after."

It is a big event. But that big event cost millions upon millions of dollars in Montreal in 1976, and residents are still paying for that Olympics.

In Atlanta, facility construction snarled the city's traffic for a couple of years before the games, and afterwards local business never reaped the benefits promised.

So, are the Olympics worth pursuing? Not to my way of thinking. But politicians and corporate leaders such as the head of General Electric (which will broadcast the next four Olympics on its NBC network) think it is worthwhile. Yet the Olympics are now more of a business bazaar than an athletic competition.

So why should New York, San Francisco, or any other place for that matter, want the Olympics? That's a good question.

City's Olympics Bid Merits a Fool's Gold Medal
Newday, New York City Edition, July 10, 2002

Here's a question for the group behind the effort to bring the 2012 Summer Olympics to New York: Why spend billions of dollars in public and private money to tie up huge areas of the city for an athletic event that lasts only 17 days a decade from now?

The founder of NYC2012, Dan Doctoroff, now the city's deputy mayor of economic development, says the answer is that the city will get a huge boost from staging the "world's greatest sporting event." But this one-time investment banker with ties to real estate developers must know that it's just a promise. Numbers on a piece of paper.

First, New York has to be designated by the United States Olympic Committee as its representative to compete against other international cities for the right to hold the 2012 games. The task force was here early last week before going to Houston and San Francisco this weekend. As we saw in Atlanta and Sydney, the International Olympic Committee prefers shiny new facilities rather than old places. Yankee Stadium, Shea Stadium, Madison Square Garden, the Nassau Coliseum and the Astoria Pool just don't cut it. Washington, San Francisco and Houston have newer facilities in place.

On Nov. 3, the USOC will announce its host nominee, and that will kick off a three-year battle against other world cities to get the International Olympic Committee's attention.

NYC2012 figures the Olympics will be "entirely privately funded" and cost about $3.3 billion to build and operate. But anyone who has ever been involved in municipal planning knows preliminary costs are often wrong. NYC2012 says it can pay for the Olympics through TV revenues, ticket sales, corporate sponsorships and licensing fees, according to its media guide. But NYC2012 shouldn't get too excited about TV revenues. There is no guarantee that American networks are looking to spend huge amounts of money for two weeks of athletic competition in 2012.

Also, what federally mandated corporate reforms will be in place by then? Corporation sponsorship of sports may change because of Enron's meltdown.

The International Olympic Committee requires that each host city have government subsidies available in the event that an Olympics loses money. Last October, while everyone's attention was riveted to Ground Zero, the New York State Legislature guaranteed up to $250 million just in case it's needed for cost overruns. New York taxpayers have become, in effect, NYC2012 partners.

NYC2012 would like to build an Olympic stadium by expanding the Jacob Javits Convention Center to add an 86,000-seat facility on the West Side of Manhattan, as part of a plan to redevelop the Hudson Yards area. NYC2012 thinks it will cost $168 million to expand the center. That seems ludicrous. Just buying the land and building a stadium platform over the rail yards could cost $300 million alone.

Then there is the "Olympic X Plan." NYC2012 envisions people using expanded water and rail service to get to each Olympic venue. The transportation scheme depends on extending the No. 7 subway line to 34th Street and the Hudson River, where the new stadium would be. It could cost an estimated $1.5 billion in public funding to redo the No. 7 line. Without the extension, the "Olympic X" transportation link, which is so critical to the plan, is dead—and so is New York's bid for the Games.

Athletes will need a place to live. Doctoroff and his people have a solution. A private development corporation will build the Queens West Athletic Village on 34 acres of land owned by the Port Authority. After the Olympics, the site will be turned over to the private sector with the hopes that it will become the cornerstone of a new neighborhood.

Who will choose the builders of the planned Olympic Village, and why wait 10 years to develop the property? If it is good enough for athletes in 2012, why not open it up for city people in 2004?

Wouldn't the city's spending billions of dollars for Olympic infrastructure have an impact on our quality of life? Does the city have the financial wherewithal to hold an Olympics, close future budget gaps, and provide educational and social services to the city's population? Doctoroff and his committee are gung-ho about the games, but who will ultimately profit? Will it be New Yorkers or private investors?

If New York City somehow manages to get the 2012 Summer Olympics, would it really benefit the city? The answer is no. New York doesn't need more international exposure. In the end, taxpayers will be forced to pick up billions of dollars worth of expenses for a luxury they can't afford: an overpriced Olympics.

Do We Really Want to Host the 2012 Olympics?
The Bergen Record, August 27, 2002

The question of whether or not New Jersey gets to host a slice of the 2012 Summer Olympics may be answered today. The United States Olympic Committee will reduce the number of cities that want the games from four to two at its Chicago meeting. New York/New Jersey is competing with Washington/Baltimore, Houston, and San Francisco.

Here's a question for the group behind the effort to bring the 2012 Summer Olympics to the area. Why bother?

Why spend billions of dollars in public and private money to tie up huge areas of the city and force changes in commuter traffic routes for an athletic event that lasts only 17 days a decade from now?

The founder of NYC2012, Dan Doctoroff, now the city's deputy mayor of economic development, says the answer is that the city will get a huge boost from staging the "world's greatest sporting event." But this one-time investment banker with ties to real estate developers must know that it's just a promise. Numbers on a piece of paper.

First, New York has to be designated by the United States Olympic Committee on Nov. 3 as its representative to compete against other international cities for the right to hold the 2012 games.

As we saw in Atlanta and Sydney, the International Olympic Committee prefers shiny new facilities rather than old places. Yankee Stadium, Shea Stadium, Giants Stadium, the Meadowlands Arena, Madison Square Garden, the Nassau Coliseum, and the Astoria Pool just don't cut it. Washington, San Francisco, and Houston have newer facilities in place.

NYC2012 figures the Olympics will be "entirely privately funded" and cost about $3.3 billion to build and operate. But anyone who has ever been involved in municipal planning knows preliminary costs are often wrong.

NYC2012 says it can pay for the Olympics through TV revenues, ticket sales, corporate sponsorships, and licensing fees, according to its media guide. But NYC2012 shouldn't get too excited about TV revenues. There is no guarantee that American networks are looking to spend huge amounts of money for two weeks of athletic competition in 2012.

The International Olympic Committee requires that each host city have government subsidies available in the event that an Olympics loses money. Last October, the New York State Legislature guaranteed up to $250 million, just in case it's needed for cost overruns. New York taxpayers have become, in effect, NYC2012 partners.

New Jersey taxpayers aren't putting up money, at least not yet. But the proposed Newark Arena could be part of the plans and Giants Stadium will be 36 years old in 2012, which is ancient by today's standards.

NYC2012 would like to build an Olympic stadium by expanding the Jacob Javits Convention Center to add an 86,000-seat facility on the West Side of Manhattan, as part of a plan to redevelop the Hudson Yards area. NYC2012 thinks it will cost $168 million to expand the center. That seems ludicrous. Just buying the land and building a stadium platform over the rail yards could cost $300 million alone.

Does the city have the financial wherewithal to hold an Olympics, close future budget gaps, and provide educational and social services to the city's population? Doctoroff and his committee are gung-ho about the games, but who will ultimately profit? Will it be New Yorkers or private investors?

There is one additional question that needs to be answered. How much security will be needed for an international event that has been a world platform for grievances in the past?

The Bush administration had more troops protecting the 2002 Salt Lake City games than in Afghanistan. How do you secure an area as densely populated as New York City, its suburbs, and northern New Jersey, and who pays for it?

If New York somehow manages to get the 2012 Summer Olympics, would it really benefit the city and New Jersey? The answer is no.

New York doesn't need more international exposure. The New Jersey component of the games seems to be afterthought. In the end, taxpayers will be forced to pick up billions of dollars worth of expenses for a luxury they can't afford: an overpriced Olympics.

We Don't Need New Arenas to Host Games
Newsday, New York City Edition, October 2, 2002

The next four weeks mark an important period for local
sports lovers—and it has nothing to do with the World Series. Will
Super Bowl and Olympic planners appreciate New York the way
international marathoners and UN delegates do, or will the National
Football League and the United States Olympic Committee leave us
flat?

The NFL could decide on Oct. 31 to place the 2007 Super Bowl
in the metropolitan area, and the United States Olympic Committee
will select its bid city for the 2012 Summer Games on Nov. 2.

And why wouldn't the NFL or the Olympics Committee not
choose New York? The NFL could put a Super Bowl at Giants
Stadium in the Meadowlands, a facility good enough to host the
1994 Soccer World Cup and attract the Army-Navy college football
game every few years. And the Olympics can take advantage of the
New York Yankees name and stage events at Yankee Stadium or
at Charles Dolan's self-described, "World's Most Famous Arena,"
Madison Square Garden. Both New York City facilities are rich in
sports lore.

But I have a feeling that New York is going to strike out twice
in three days. And it's not because the city doesn't have the financial
wherewithal or the fan interest to hold both events. It does. What
New York doesn't have is a shiny, new stadium, complete with the
requisite luxury suites and club seating that sports owners and
organizations favor—and that's the problem.

The National Football League will hold its annual fall meeting
on Oct. 30 and 31 in Manhattan. The league could give New York
a Super Bowl on either day, but the lack of a new stadium and our
February winter weather are major drawbacks.

Some of the NFL's most memorable title games have been played
in real winter conditions, such as last year's AFC Championship
Game in the snow in Foxboro, Mass., the Ice Bowl in Green Bay in
1967, and the extreme Yankee Stadium cold in December, 1962 (9
degrees above zero). But today's NFL owners have grown soft and
don't seem very keen on risking a week's worth of golf and parties in

the warm February sun of Florida, Arizona, Louisiana or California in exchange for the cold, snow and ice of frigid New York.

The NFL requires that a Super Bowl host city with an outdoor stadium have an average daily February temperature of over 50 degrees. New York's 33-degree average just isn't suitable for hitting the links.

Right now, the area's only Super Bowl-ready venue is Giants Stadium, which is still in good structural shape. But it's going to be 31 years old come 2007 and that means it will have to be renovated. The NFL, by awarding New York a Super Bowl, could provide the catalyst needed to start construction on a West Side football stadium, which could also be used for the 2012 Summer Olympics.

There doesn't seem to be much of a rush to get a stadium built on the West Side except at the New York Jets headquarters and Deputy Mayor Dan Doctoroff's office, both in Manhattan. Doctoroff is the founder of NYC2012, the group behind the drive to bring the Olympics to the city. The proposed West Side stadium hasn't surfaced as much of an issue in this year's gubernatorial race. Gov. George Pataki seems to be willing to invest in a West Side stadium, while Comptroller H. Carl McCall has come out against it. Tom Golisano is mum on this question.

But the venue for these games could become a hot topic should New York City somehow be selected to host the Super Bowl and if it advances to the final round of bidding for the 2012 Summer Games. Then stadium building and funding will become a major agenda item. A West Side stadium could wind up costing more than a billion dollars— and that's a lot of construction contracts to award some lucky bidder (and generous campaign contributor).

Back in the early 1980s, the International Olympic Committee was so desperate to stage a successful 1984 Summer Olympics that it waived all of its building requirements for the Los Angeles games. NFL Commissioner Paul Tagliabue says he wants to help our local economy continue to rebuild after the 9/11 World Trade Center attack. Therefore, both the NFL and the International Olympic Committee, assuming it picks the city, should take the area's stadiums and arenas as they are and not ask the public to pay for new ones.

New York will probably lose out on both the Super Bowl and the Olympics because world-famous sports venues won't sway narcissistic sports barons who are more interested in expensive, glitzy buildings for their own gratification than what New York has to offer. Too bad for them—it's their loss, not ours.

Baseball May Be Out of 'Our' 2012 Olympics
Newsday, New York City Edition, November 26, 2002

Forget football for a moment and think of the future. Imagine a 2012 Summer Olympics in New York: world-class athletes competing for the gold in 28 Olympic sports in shiny, expensive and, in most cases, taxpayer-supported new facilities throughout the city.

All sports, that is, except baseball.

This Thanksgiving the International Olympic Committee, meeting in Mexico City between tomorrow and Friday, could give baseball fans a bad call: no baseball in the Olympics starting possibly as early as the 2008 Games in Beijing.

All it takes is a simple majority of the 120 IOC delegates to go along with an IOC programs committee recommendation that baseball, softball, Greco-Roman wrestling and the modern pentathlon be eliminated.

The IOC would replace those four sports with golf and rugby. That might be good news for Bethpage Black or Winged Foot, or for the handful of dedicated rugby players in our area. But the Mets and Yankees sell more than 5 million tickets between them, and when you throw in another half million sold by the Brooklyn Cyclones and the Staten Island Yankees, you realize that the International Olympic Committee doesn't really know much about New Yorkers' love of baseball.

Neither golf nor rugby gets the blood flowing here like a George Steinbrenner deal or the Mets' latest blunder.

Of course, baseball has never been much of an Olympic sport. In 1984, the United States played in an Olympic exhibition series and lost to Japan, despite having Mark McGwire, Barry Larkin and Will Clark in our lineup—all relative unknowns at the time. In 2000, Tommy Lasorda led a patchwork team of college all-stars and some former big leaguers to Olympic gold by beating Cuba.

The IOC wants big-time players in the Olympics, like the NBA's Dream Team back in 1984. The IOC wants marquee names like Barry Bonds, Roger Clemens, Mike Piazza, Alex Rodriguez and

Derek Jeter. But Major League Baseball won't let those players go to the Summer Olympics because it doesn't want to interrupt the season.

Remember, the Olympics are all about money. College players and has-beens don't cut it. The 2000 U.S.A. baseball team won the gold, but it didn't bring in the cash. So, instead of allowing fans to root for a bunch of players trying to make a name for themselves, the IOC wants established names, so it can sell them to their corporate partners. It's not about athletic competition any more or being fan friendly.

Maybe by dropping America's pastime, the IOC figures it can get back at the United States for being too powerful and too wealthy. Meanwhile former IOC President Juan Antonio Samaranch thinks that New York City is a front-runner, and that makes sense considering American TV networks pay huge sums to get broadcast rights, American companies are IOC corporate partners and sponsors, and Americans buy a lot of Olympic-related merchandise.

Some members of the IOC may dislike New York as a potential host city, but they sure do like American dollars.

And speaking of American dollars, why is there a single-minded desire by the Bloomberg administration to get these games, which are so costly (an estimated $6 billion and counting) and whose construction and subway extension will literally stop traffic for years and years prior to the 17-day Olympic gathering? Has Mayor Michael Bloomberg forgotten that the Mets and the Yankees want new stadiums, or is this Olympic scheme part of a grand plan that will give the Yankees, the Mets, the Knicks and the Rangers new facilities while bringing the Jets back across the Hudson River?

Those are just two questions that Bloomberg and Deputy Mayor Daniel Doctoroff have to answer. What is the real reason for bringing the Olympics to town? It can't be the "it's good for New York" mantra.

Do Bloomberg and Doctoroff honestly think the Olympics will really improve the quality of life, create an economic engine that will create real and permanent jobs, and improve New York's standing in the international community? Or is hosting the Olympics an economic opportunity for just a handful of people?

And one other thing that bothers me about the New York Olympics bid: Why haven't Bloomberg or Doctoroff publicly told the IOC that it better have baseball in our Olympics? After all, baseball is our game.

Bad Timing for NY-NJ Olympics Bid
Bergen Record, July 25, 2003

Many of the Olympics committee voting members come from countries that have grievances with the Bush administration. The race for the 2012 Summer Olympic Games has started as nine countries have submitted proposals to the International Olympic Committee outlining their plans to host the Games. New York is one of the nine bidders and the timing of the beginning of the two-year sprint to convince the IOC that the city and Northern New Jersey are perfect hosts could not be worse from an international standpoint.

The International Olympic Committee will award the 2012 Games on July 6, 2005. So the New York Olympic Committee has two years to persuade more than 100 countries that it is the perfect place to hold an Olympics.

But many of the IOC voting members come from countries that have grievances with the Bush administration on numerous issues from rejecting the Kyoto Treaty to the Iraq War. Those voters could summarily dismiss New York not on the basis of its proposal, but on the basis of their perception of our government's policies.

That may carry far more weight in determining who gets the 2012 Summer Games than the IOC's recent decision to give Vancouver, Canada, the 2010 Winter Olympics. There is a theory that the IOC will not award a continent consecutive Olympics, but that isn't true as Athens will host the 2004 Summer Games and Turin, Italy has the 2006 Games. Another theory making the rounds is that New York won't get the 2012 Summer Games because the United States has hosted the Olympics four times since 1980. But that shouldn't be much of a factor when you consider how much money American television, General Electric's NBC unit, is giving to the IOC for the broadcast rights to the 2010 and 2012 events.

NBC would prefer to show the Games in real time in the United States, which is what Vancouver and a New York Olympics will offer. Money talks in sports, particularly in Olympic bidding.

New York's competition will come from Havana, Istanbul, Leipzig (Germany), London, Madrid, Moscow, Paris, and Rio de Janeiro.

The list of nations is both interesting and intriguing. The United States and the United Kingdom were, of course, the only coalition partners who fought in the Iraq war. France, Germany, and Russia opposed the Iraq military action. But Paris was an International Olympic Committee favorite before the Iraq action and remains that way.

The most intriguing bid will come from Havana.

How can one of the world's poorest countries bid for an Olympics that will cost billions upon billions of dollars? But Cuba's bid may signal that Fidel Castro wants to get involved with the world's business community.

There is no way that Cuba can win the bid, but Cuba could be using the Olympics as a negotiating ploy to get the United States to drop economic sanctions against the country.

The Olympics are more than an athletic competition. The Olympics are a corporate bazaar where multi-national corporations show off their products in a 17-day advertising campaign that is televised worldwide. The Olympics also provide a political platform for many groups who are looking to move up in the world order or air grievances.

So there are a few ways of looking at the Cuban decision. Cuba wants the Games for whatever prestige it would bring. But more importantly, politically and economically, Cuba wants to join the rest of the world. The Havana government may be using China as an example. China is hosting the 2008 Games and has to open its borders and its government to the world.

China is also investing billions to put its best foot forward.

The International Olympic Committee will take about two years to sift through the various bids, and this could be a highly charged and emotional decision because of the Bush administration's dealings with Iraq. There was a huge split in the United Nations' 15-member Security Council about disarming Iraq with force. A good many of those countries along with the other governments who were opposed to military action in Iraq are International Olympic Committee members and will vote in this process.

The New York Olympic Committee may feel its has the best chance of landing the Games, but it may find out that politics and diplomacy—and not a strong bid—are much more important when these Games are awarded.

Ueberroth's Appointment Has Effect on NYC 2012 Bid
Metro, June 21, 2004

For the backers of the 2012 New York Summer Olympics to bid, Peter Ueberroth's appointment as the Chairman of the United States Olympic Committee is both a plus and a problem.

The positive is that Ueberroth took a bad situation, the 1984 Los Angeles Olympics, and turned it into a money making proposition and that might help the New York bid committee with the International Olympic Committee delegates who will vote on the 2012 Olympic venue next July.

The negative for New York is that Uerberroth made money because Los Angeles didn't have to build any new facilities for the Games. Ueberroth received all sorts of accolades for holding a successful Olympics after the 1972 Munich terrorist attack which killed 11 Israeli athletes, the 1976 Montréal Olympics financial fiasco and the 1980 American boycott of the Moscow Games because of the Soviet Union's invasion of Afghanistan.

NYC2012, the New York organizing committee, originally contended that a 2012 Summer Games would cost some $3.3 billion to hold and that the Games would somehow pay for themselves with TV and licensing money providing the bulk of the necessary funding. But that was long before construction materials started to rise in cost. Simply put, the price of steel is rising.

Recently, there have been warnings from Athens that New York politicians should be seriously considering. No one knows just how much the 2004 Athens Games will really cost. The original $5.5 billion price tag has grown by at least a billion dollars.

The cost of security is absolutely staggering and other issues are already marring this summer's event. Already, the IOC President Jacques Rogge may have his final words ready for the closing ceremonies, "well, I might start by saying that these were not the best ever Games, but…"

Rogge is blaming the Greek Olympic backers for ruining his organization's biggest event because of overspending and delayed preparations.

In 1997, the then-in-power Greek Socialist party thought the Games would cost around $5.5 billion. The new Greek Government led by conservatives is claiming that the Games could possibly end up costing as much as $10 billion. Rogge recently told Belgium's *Le Soir* newspaper, "We regret this. The Greeks will have to take a long look at this after the Games."

Maybe it is time that New Yorkers also take a long look at the bid. Ueberroth thinks New York would be a great place to hold the Olympics and it could be.

Unfortunately, the best chance would be using Ueberroth's LA formula of not paying top dollar for construction. But with the IOC's requirement of brand new facilities, what are the chances of that?

Olympics About More Than Sports
Metro [Philly], August 10, 2004

Are American athletes who are going to Athens for the 2004 Summer Games there to A) fight a war; B) sell hamburgers, sneakers, soda and other items; C) prove they are not taking performance enhancing designer drugs; D) compete in an athletic competition or E) all of the above.

It appears security and drug issues will overshadow everything else that will be going on in Athens. The cost of defending Athens and Greece between now and Oct. 5 when the Paralympics Games end is more than $1.5 billion.

The Greeks plan to use Patriot Missiles to shoot down planes or other possible airborne threats if need be. The United States, along with other countries, has plans to evacuate its athletes in the event of an attack. NATO and the United States are supplying spy aircraft, there is a blimp hovering over Athens that comes complete with sophisticated sensors, and the Greek Air Force is flying constant patrols.

In fact, it seems that intelligence agencies are so sure that some group (not necessarily Al-Qaeda) will attempt to attack the Games that training to stop terrorists has become an Olympic event.

Of course, the athletes are also there to sell shoes, hamburgers, soda, watches and all the other items that have the official interlocking five rings endorsement. That is what the Olympics have become: a corporate bazaar where just about anything and everything is for sale.

The companies who have invested big sponsorship dollars may have a problem pushing their wares in Athens this year. Greeks seem to be ignoring the Olympics if ticket sales are any indication of the degree of interest the host country's citizens have. Tons of tickets to events are still available.

Maybe some of the tickets are available because Olympic officials have done such a good job casting a cloud over certain athletes who have been accused of taking designer drugs. People want to be entertained and the best entertainment has come from people like Marion Jones who has accused anti-doping agencies of smearing her.

There is a nine-page World Anti-Doping Code that team doctors carry around and the doctors have to be careful what they prescribe if an athlete gets a cold or runs a fever. At the 2000 Sydney Games, 16-year-old Romanian Gold Medalist Andreea Raducan lost her all-around gold medal when she tested positive for pseudoephedrine, a banned stimulant that is in a cold medicine. She took the cold remedy after it was prescribed by a Romanian official.

Yes, this is an athletic competition and for some, not people like Allen Iverson, the Olympics are a once in a lifetime event. Unfortunately, the archer who spent his or her life to get to the pinnacle will be overshadowed by the United States Olympic Basketball Team or the Williams Sisters in tennis, which leads to a few questions.

The Olympics end at the beginning of tennis's US Open in New York. Is an Olympic Gold more valuable to the Williams' sisters than winning the Flushing Meadows tournament? Is the pursuit of winning an Olympic Gold Medal for Iverson more important than the 2004–05 NBA season for Iverson?

One answer that seems crystal clear is that selling merchandise is more important than competition. Maybe that's why millions of tickets have not yet been sold at this year's Games.

Stadium Costs Rarely Add Up, Even After Olympics
Metro, August 16, 2004

As New York City Mayor Michael Bloomberg continues to push for the construction of a football/Olympics stadium on Manhattan's west side, both he and New York Gov. George Pataki should be aware of the fiscal drain that is occurring in Houston, Texas, after the city partnered with local teams to build new sports facilities.

The new stadiums did bring events: Houston did hold the Super Bowl in its new football stadium last February and baseball's All-Star Game was played in the city's new stadium.

But while the sports world was focusing on the two major crown jewel events, the Harris County-Houston Sports Authority was looking to find money to pay off the debt on the baseball park, football stadium and arena.

When Houston Mayor Lee Brown, a former NYC Police Commissioner, along with the rest of his administration was doing due diligence on the costs of building new sports facilities, he figured that a hike in hotel and motel room sales taxes along with an increase in rent-a-car taxes would pay for the construction.

But the Brown administration did not foresee an economic downturn. The Harris County-Houston Sports Authority has experienced a decline in tourism tax revenues since the Sept. 11 terrorist attacks. Instead of an annual anticipated 3 percent hike in collecting tourism tax revenues, Houston has lost about 10 percent of its sports facilities tax monies in 2002 and in 2003.

The Harris County-Houston Sports Authority is now issuing some $37.2 million in bonds to help pay off the costs of construction. That was not how Brown envisioned the future when taxpayers were asked to vote yes on various referendums to build the sports structures.

Houston kept its major league sports status, but its taxpayers are paying more money for sports, and some services and programs are going to lose funding so that the city can pay its sports debts.

Bloomberg and Pataki look at a stadium as an economic engine and as the centerpiece for the 2012 Summer Olympics. But the

2004 Athens Olympics have been a financial disaster for the Greek government, and another international sporting event in 2002 didn't turn out the way Japanese and South Korean officials had hoped. Soccer's 2002 World Cup has left behind a number of useless soccer stadiums in both countries. The Sydney, Australia Olympics is still costing taxpayers money and left behind a number of useless facilities.

Bloomberg keeps pushing the West Side stadium but history suggests that overestimated revenues and underestimated costs won't add up for New York taxpayers.

Fans and the Public

"What Do People Want from Sports Today? Just Ask Them"

Street & Smiths' Sportsbusiness Journal, January 24–30, 2000

What do people want from sports today? As someone who gives speeches and lectures about the business and politics of sports before college kids, young adults, middle-aged adults and senior citizens, I ask that question. The answers from across the board are generally the same.

People want good entertainment value for their money but feel cheated today.

The No. 1 complaint is the cost of tickets and how expensive it is for a family to see a major league contest. Second, those who have attended my speeches say there is too much inconvenience in physically attending games.

People don't like the loud, continuous music and the fact that team owners think a game experience should include ear-splitting music, sideshows and boorish actions by fans that in theory give a hometown team an edge. In fact, people have told me after my speeches that games are supposed to be a leisurely activity and for the most part have become hard to attend for numerous reasons.

People 35 and older don't like the fact that they cannot discuss any aspect of a game during any dead moment because some programmer has turned up some heavy metal song to the noise level of a jet taking off at an airport.

People don't like boorish behavior of young people who seem to use the excuse of going to a sporting event to get drunk and spit out mean-spirited, foul-mouthed obscenities or start fights with others.

Others don't like all the sideshow aspects connected with the presentation of the game because it interferes with their intent of watching a baseball, football, basketball, hockey, or soccer game. That includes shooting T-shirts into a crowd where people jump over one another for a chance at getting one of those prized garments. That includes people dressed in sumo wrestler suits fighting at center ice between periods at hockey games.

People don't mind seeing kid hockey players having a mini game between periods at hockey games or Punt, Pass and Kick contests at halftime of football games. That's not artificial entertainment. People don't like the ersatz quality of most sideshow promotions that teams run today.

People do tell me boxing and track and field offer events to watch without the sideshow. Even though boxing is a sideshow in itself with its bikini or swimsuit-clad card women, still, the action in the ring is the thing.

Some people are very interested in how their taxes go to support stadiums and arenas and how the general public is left out of the public financing debate for athletic venues.

There are a few hecklers here and there who tell me I don't know what I am talking about. That's fine. They are entitled to their opinion as long as I am entitled to mine. And I don't mind the hecklers as long as they realize I get paid and they don't.

College-aged people accept sports as a business these days with grievances, threats of franchise relocation, strikes and lockout as parts of the sports landscape. They aren't bothered by the turmoil because they don't know anything else. Some of them weren't even born when baseball shut down during the 1981 player walkout.

People 35 and older are resentful of the high salaries and the business aspect of the sports industry.

I do get a cross-section of people in my audiences, some sports fans and some not. The non-sports fans seem to have the most curiosity about the business and politics of sports. They don't go to the game yet are paying for it through government financing of arenas and stadiums.

In downstate New York, people wonder why their taxes go to upstate New York for minor league venues in Buffalo, Syracuse, Rochester, Binghamton and Albany. People in Michigan wonder why, when they went to Seattle, Tampa, Miami and Texas, they paid extra car rental and hotel/motel and restaurant taxes for venues that they probably will never use.

Peter Ueberroth once told me never to underestimate the intelligence of the public. I think sports operators should forget about focus and research groups and head to a library, a local Y, a senior citizens home, or a college and give a talk. They might be surprised by some of the feedback they get and might listen to people who are not screened and eliminated by some focus coordinator. They actually could learn something from the average person—who might really be a paying customer.

Fight Back with the Pocketbook

The Baltimore Sun, unpublished, 2002

This article was edited, ready to go and pulled at the last minute because higher ups at the Sun said the paper did not support boycotts.

If you listen to sports talk radio or read writers from all walks of life writing about a possible baseball strike, there is a sense of resignation: The fans are saps with no voice who are hopelessly devoted to baseball.

Simply put, baseball fans have no control over the situation in the spat between multi-millionaire owners and millionaire players if and when the players walk out.

But baseball fans should know they can fight back and hit both sides hard where it hurts—the pocketbook.

And here's how the fans can mount a counteroffensive:

- They should contact their state attorney general's office and make sure a mechanism is in place to ensure that they get refunds from games missed on cable TV. The refunds to the country's 86 million cable subscribers, who receive sports channels even if they don't want them, should come from the cable TV owners who transmit the baseball games. In Baltimore, that's Comcast, because it has the rights to show the Orioles.

- Fans should call their local, not national, elected officials. In those cities where the municipality helped to pay for a new baseball stadium, make sure that the team continues to pay rent during a baseball work stoppage. Municipalities should sue if a team withholds its rent because games were canceled.

Baseball fans have enormous power; all they have to do is act. There's the all-time favorite, the boycott.

For example, if fans are upset with San Francisco Giants owner Peter McGowan, don't shop at Safeway; he's a director of the supermarket's board after having been its chairman and CEO. If Dodger fans don't like Rupert Murdoch's role in the baseball stalemate, they don't have to watch the Fox network or go to movies produced by 20th Century Fox.

Hungry and want some pizza? Don't buy Detroit Tiger owner Mike Ilitch's Little Caesar's products.

Looking to go to a theme park in Orlando, Fla., or southern California? Scratch the Disney parks in either locale. Also don't watch ESPN, ESPN2, ESPNews, ESPN Classic, listen to ESPN Radio or see any Disney movies. The Walt Disney Co. owns the Anaheim Angels.

The media? AOL-Time Warner owns the Atlanta Braves. You can drop AOL as your Internet provider and seek another one. You don't have to buy *Sports Illustrated, Time* or *People*, watch CNN or *CNN Headline News*, the Cartoon Channel, HBO or go to New Line Cinema movies, buy Kodak products or spend a day at Warner Brothers Recreation Enterprises and theme parks or buy Atlantic Records products.

Check stadium names. Budweiser, or Busch Stadium (St. Louis), Coors Field (Denver), Miller Park (Milwaukee), Minute Maid Field (Houston), Tropicana Field (St. Petersburg) are spending millions on partnerships, but there are other beers and juices to drink.

Bank One (Phoenix), Comerica (Detroit) and PNC (Pittsburgh) aren't the only financial institutions around. Edison (Anaheim) and Cinergy (Cincinnati) are just two energy companies available. Network Associates (Oakland) and Qualcomm (San Diego) are just two of many technology companies. Don't shop at Safeco (Seattle).

Fans don't need to buy baseball cards, which puts money into players' pockets, nor do they need to attend baseball card shows or stand in line for autographs.

Fans should boycott buying licensed products and keep their money in their pockets instead of lining the pockets of both players and owners.

Sure, fans can boycott a game here and there and make a minor stand. But that won't send any messages to the owners and players who continue to bicker over how to split up billions of dollars.

Some 70 million people attend Major League baseball games annually. Millions watch them on TV or listen to them on the radio. If just a fraction of that audience reacts, both the owners and players will get the message, and it could force a settlement in a hurry.

What's Wrong With Baseball? Nothing
NBCSports.com, March 30, 2005

Sometime around 8 p.m. eastern time on Sunday, the Voice of Yankee Stadium—Bob Shepherd —will welcome fans to the Bronx ballyard. Shepherd's introduction of the 2004 World Champion Boston Red Sox will bring on a chorus of boos along with innovative and colorful language from the more than 55,000 humans in the House That Ruth Built.

Baseball is back, not that it ever left. Baseball is the most resilient of businesses.

BALCO? No big deal to its customer base. Congressional hearings on steroid use by players? Who cares? Threats of contracting two teams coming just 48 hours after the 2001 World Series? Not a concern. Players strike canceling the 1994 World Series? Momentarily upset but no lasting scars. Owners collusion in the 1980s? Stuff happens.

Baseball fans don't care. It's all about how far the ball goes over the fence and who hit it. That's what baseball fans care about, entertainment.

There are no ethics when it comes to baseball and sports. There is no shame except for a few sportswriters and radio talk show hosts who complain that Mark McGwire looked bad before a Congressional committee.

Baseball may have been slightly tarnished by Jose Canseco's book, but it's not really going to suffer as an industry. Just look at what has happened since the first news of the San Francisco Grand Jury looking into what was going on with BALCO broke.

Major League Baseball held an auction for its ownerless and orphaned Montreal franchise. Washington, D.C. Mayor Anthony Williams apparently thought he was in a real contest to get the franchise and wrest it away from Portland and Las Vegas. So Williams gave Major League Baseball what the industry wanted. A taxpayer-funded $600 million ballpark and handing baseball virtually all of the revenue generated within the facility. Williams and the Washington, D.C. City Council were apparently not bothered by baseball's steroid scandal.

XM Satellite Radio signed a multi-million dollar deal with Major League Baseball after the San Francisco Grand Jury listened to Barry Bonds, Jason Giambi, Gary Sheffield and others testify about their relationship with BALCO.

The New York Mets signed a partnership deal with Comcast and Time Warner to start a New York regional sports network beginning in 2006. Comcast could also be partners with Major League Baseball and place the Washington Nationals on its regional sports network in the Mid-Atlantic states should Commissioner Bud Selig and his associates ever cut a deal with Baltimore Orioles owner Peter Angelos that would allow Nationals games on cable and over-the-air TV. Comcast also started a regional Chicago sports network partnering with the Chicago Tribune Company, the owners of the Cubs, Jerry Reinsdorf who owns the White Sox and Bulls and Bill Wirtz, the Blackhawks owner.

Las Vegas Mayor Oscar Goodman went to the Winter Meetings in Anaheim looking for a team, and has some talks with the Florida Marlins ownership about moving to the Nevada city. Goodman also claimed that another franchise might have some interest in moving to his city. Miami elected officials are still in serious negotiations trying to figure out how much taxpayer money should be used in building a new baseball park for the Marlins.

Minnesota Governor Tim Pawlenty and the state legislature are also trying to come up with a plan to build a new baseball park for the Twins.

General Motors just signed a three-year sponsorship deal with the game. Major League Baseball's marketing partners have not left. It's business as usual.

If Major League Baseball is so scandal ridden, why are politicians spending taxpayers money like drunken sailors on a weekend leave? If Major League Baseball has a weak public image because of alleged steroid abuse by some players, why are advertisers pumping millions of dollars into baseball advertising? Why are cable operators like Comcast and Time Warner so eager to partner with Major League Baseball?

If people were really fed up, they would not be handing out $600 million stadiums to Major League Baseball. Satellite radio networks along with cable TV and over-the-air networks would be demanding changes in their contracts or just canceling them.

Cities and states would be demanding changes in their leases with teams at taxpayer-funded stadiums that were built.

None of this has happened. Cities are spending billions for facilities in both Major League and Minor League Baseball. TV and radio networks are still giving baseball teams billions of dollars; advertisers still want to be associated with Major League Baseball. It's the big leagues after all, the best.

People want to be associated with the sport. People want autographs and want to be entertained. People want baseball.